The Small and Medium Enterprise Ecosystem in Ethiopia

The Small and Medium Enterprise Ecosystem in Ethiopia

The Impact of Innovative Finance for improvement of the Manufacturing Sector

Ajebush Argaw Shafi

&

Mammo Muchie

RSP

THE RED SEA PRESS

TRENTON | LONDON | NEW DELHI | CAPE TOWN | NAIROBI | ADDIS ABABA | ASMARA | IBADAN

THE RED SEA PRESS
541 West Ingham Avenue | Suite B
Trenton, New Jersey 08638

Book and cover design: Lemlem Tadesse

Cataloging-in-Publication Data may be obtained from the Library of Congress.

ISBNs: 978-1-56902-770-7 HB
978-1-56902-771-4 PB

Dedication

To Ethiopia to enter into the innovation era entirely freed from ethnic distractions

TABLE OF CONTENTS

PREFACE

Economic wealth, aside from farming output, is created through enterprises. When economists, policy makers, and ordinary citizens talk about the growth of the economy, they are mostly talking about the expansion of enterprise output. Large firms contribute substantially to economic growth and wealth creation but the aggregate contribution of small and medium-sized enterprises (SMEs) is also considerable— in some countries, it is greater than that of large enterprises. Along with output, SMEs create jobs, make investments, and export their goods to foreign markets. Dynamic and innovative SMEs expand the technological frontiers of their sector and their country.

Despite their contribution, smaller firms face many barriers. Some barriers arise from government regulations that disproportionately hamper smaller firms. However, there are also barriers inherent in markets that affect enterprises because of their size. These barriers we call "size-induced market failures" and they occur in the key areas that affect enterprise competitiveness. Failures in the markets for credit, technology, and skilled workers, along with difficulty in accessing domestic and international markets, are the main areas for concern. Information asymmetries in some markets, notably for finance, are a major obstacle, as are the disproportionately higher costs that SMEs face in accessing credit and other markets.

Policy makers throughout Asia have sought to address these failures through policies and programs that assist SMEs. This book is about identifying and understanding key market failures and assessing the efforts of government in addressing them. The book comprises studies presented at the workshop on SMEs in Developing Asia: New Approaches to Overcoming Market Failures held on 19–20 November 2015 at our institute in Tokyo. We were happy to organize this event in collaboration with three Japanese organizations: the SME Agency of the Ministry of Finance, the Japan International Cooperation Agency (JICA) Research Institute, and the Credit Risk Database Association.

The chapters contained herein will contribute to a better understanding of SME constraints and lead to improved policy learning to transform, perform, reform and make sustainable economic development in Ethiopia and the rest of the Global South.

This book analyses the dynamic and transformative nature of Ethiopian manufacturing firm in recent period using establishment level of individual census panel data from 2005-2014. Four related topics such as: Analysing Firm age and size as Determinants of Business Success in Ethiopian Manufacturing Sector, Factors for Manufacturing Enterprises Success, Access to loan and Manufacturing Enterprises Performance in a Developing Country,

Part 1 provides empirical evidence on the relationships between firm age, size and manufacturing firm's success. Tries to address the concern of how and to what extent firm age and size matter on business success and it has been in interest of many practitioners, researchers and policy makers. This study therefore, pursues to understand the influence of firm ages and size on business success. The empirical analysis of this research work is based on Ethiopian large and medium manufacturing census survey data 2005-2014 conducted by central statistics agency of the country. The study follows Evans (1987a, 1987b), view for specifying the relationship between firm ages, size and manufacturing enterprises success in terms of profit growth. Firm's profit growth considered as potential business success indicators and applies inferential statistical techniques such as '*Ordinary Least Square*' (OLS) for measuring the significance level and multivariate analysis to test the hypothesis of association. The result indicates that there is a negative and statistically significant relationship between firm ages, size and business success in terms of profit growth. In other words, our empirical results indicate that business success decreases with firm size and age. Smaller and younger firms have better profit performance than bigger and older firms do. The study helps to resolve the previous conflicting empirical evidence on the area. Therefore, the findings contributed to the often contradictory and inconclusive literatures on firm age and size impact on manufacturing enterprises profit.

Part 2 This study analyses and determines the influence of finance access on the Small and Medium Enterprises (SMEs) performance in Ethiopia. Samples of 1,542 out of the population of 2,682 SMEs are drawn from the Ethiopian Manufacturing Enterprise survey data for the years 2005-2012 in an explanatory study. The study follows Slow's growth theory (1957) for specifying the relationship between inputs, efficiency and outputs using 'Cobb- Douglass production function'. In addition, a linear, dynamic mathematical model is used to estimate SMEs profitability. The study also applies average treatment effect (ATE) to evaluate the influence of credit on the SMEs performance as Rosenbaum & Rubin (1983) have done it. The study also applied inferential statistical techniques such as 'Ordinary Least Square' (OLS) for measuring the significance level and multivariate analysis to test the hypothesis of association. The key findings are; SMEs that are running by individuals who have access to bank credit have a higher level of 'Total Factor Productivity'. More precisely, average TFP among enterprises with access to bank credit is 1.25 times higher than enterprises without bank credit and the results are statistically significant. The study also found a negative but

statistically insignificant relationship between access to bank loan and
SMEs profitability.

Part 3 examines Small and Medium Enterprises productivity performance as a factor of access to credit within the Ethiopian economy. Empirical analysis is based on Ethiopian Large and Medium Manufacturing Enterprise survey (LMMIS) data 2005-2011. Precisely, the research aims to understand whether SMEs with access to bank credit have higher levels of total factor productivity (TFP) relative to counterparts without access to credit. To address this objective the study uses fixed effect regression modelling and neoclassical production function for specifying the relationship between inputs, efficiency and outputs. The study also applies inferential statistical techniques such as OLS (ordinary least square) for measuring the significance level and multivariate analysis to test the hypotheses of association. The following main conclusions can be drawn from the study. The study proves that SMEs that are run by individuals who have access to bank credit have a higher level of TFP. More precisely, average TFP among enterprises with access to bank credit is 1.3 times higher than enterprises with no access.

ACKNOWLEDGMENTS

Sincere appreciation for the approval to use the statistical data from Ethiopia and the support from DSI/NRF SARChI in Industrial Engineering at Tshwane University of Technology.

CHAPTER 1: INTRODUCTION

The productivity and profitability of manufacturing enterprises in developing countries, appears to be extremely low in comparison to their counterparts in the developed world (Abegaz, 2013; Bloom *et al.*, 2010; Lanjouw and Lanjouw, 2001; Tybout, 2000). This attribute of low-performance is especially common among Small and Medium Enterprises (SMEs). Despite this reality, in low-income countries there is great interest in SME development as a major tool of poverty reduction (Abegaz, 2013).

Various studies including Lora & Pagés (2011); Robb *et al.* (2012); Bigsten & Gebreeyesus (2007); Badia and Slootmaekers, (2008), have found that in developing countries there are many constraints on the growth of potentially productive SMEs, such that they cannot expand, and cannot make technological improvements that are needed to increase productivity performance. World Bank (2015) enterprises survey result shows that the biggest business obstacle for SMEs was lack of access to finance.

Dalberg (2011) reports that 41 percent of SMEs in developing countries reveal access to finance as a significant constraint to growth and development, while this figure is only 30 percent of SMEs in middle-income countries, and only 15 percent of SMEs in high-income countries. Brixiova (2009) shows that small and medium enterprises are more bank credit constrained in their operation than other category of firms. Beck *et al.* (2008) mentioned finance as a key determinant of resources and motivations for SME growth and performance in terms of its productivity and profitability. According to Abdullah *et al.* (2011), the ability of SMEs to fulfil their potential contribution in an economy depends on the level and accessibility of finance. This implies that access to credit should can enable SMEs to improve productivity performance. Access to external finance like bank credit may allow firms to have better capacity to acquire necessary working capital and technical inputs that could have favourable impacts on SMEs' productivity and growth patterns (Bouri *et al.*, 2011, Nagler & Naudé, 2014). In other words, credit allows SMEs to invest beyond what their internal funds can support

Despite the great emphasis on financial constraints in the SME study, the empirical literature on the link between finance and enterprises performance is scant. Most studies focus on the role of financial development and economic growth. For example, at the macro level Beck *et al.* (2000) show that financial intermediaries help economic growth through more efficient resource allocation rather than through investment or saving. Arestis *et al.* (2003) argue that financial policies affect growth mainly through total factor productivity (TFP).

Although these previous researches addressed various aspects on financial development or access to finance, they put little attention or emphasis on the direct effect of finance constraints on SMEs productivity and profitability performances. Moreover, the focus of much of the literatures (Siedschlag *et al.*, 2014; Stierwald, 2010; Love and Zicchino, 2006; Rioja and Valev, 2004) are limited to large and stock market-listed firms in developed world, with little attention given to small and medium enterprises in the developing countries that perhaps are mostly affected by credit constraint.

This study contributes to the SME literature by investigating the direct effects of access to bank credit on SME productivity and profitability performance in Ethiopia. The study utilizes manufacturing industry survey data collected by the Ethiopian Central Statistical Agency (CSA) over the period of 2005 to

2012. It adopts a fixed effect model, panel data estimators and takes SMEs total factor productivity as a partial productivity measure and as a proxy for enterprise performance.

The study explicitly addresses the ongoing statistical concerns in the SMEs productivity and profitability performance models such as sample censoring and regression on the mean and unobserved heterogeneity. More precisely the study helps to understand how the typical value of the productivity and profitability of SMEs changes, when one of the variables such as access to bank credit is varied while the other independent variables are fixed.

Despite the tremendous efforts made to improve the performances of manufacturing SMEs in developing countries particularly in Ethiopia, the growth and contributions of the sector remains beleaguered. Among the multiple factors for this low performance of SMEs, the lack of access to formal credit and inadequate financial services remain the top obstacles. There is also great emphasis on SMEs financial constraints in the literature (Kuntchev *et al.*, 2012; Berg, *et al.*, 2012; World Bank, 2015; Carpnter and Bruce, 2002; Beck *et al.,* 2007) however, there is limited empirical evidence on the link between access to finance and the SMEs productivity and profitability especially in developing country context (Lashitew, 2011).

There are also studies (for example Wurgler, 2000; Love, 2003; Gebrehiwot & Wolday, 2006; Nichter and Goldmark, 2009; Fagan and Zhao, 2009; Atieno, 2009) emphasising the importance of access to finance for SMEs performance. However, there are also limited sources that explore the link between manufacturing SMEs performance and finance development (Abegaz, 2013) and less attention has been given to establish whether access to bank credit improves the performance of SMEs. Moreover, existing empirical studies (e.g. Beck *et al.,* 2007; Dinh *et al.,* 2010; Butler and Cornaggia, 2007) have been conducted in the area of finance and SMEs performance from developed countries context and very few studies have focused on the developing nations (e.g Gatti and

Love, 2006; Lashitew, 2011; Olutunla and Obamuyi, 2008). A few empirical studies (see Reyes *et al.*, 2012; Ghani & Suri, 1999; Hanson, 2001; Malesky & Taussig, 2009; Allen *et al.,* 2012) on the area of investigating the influence of access to finance on firms' performance; the findings are not always consistent in terms of the directions of the association between bank credit and firms' performance. According to Nkurunziza (2010), use of bank credit can have a positive and significant impact on firm performance if it helps the firm address its liquidity constraints, or it can have a negative impact when there are shocks in the economy leading to increased interest rates.

Graham and Leary (2011) argued that, although various studies have been done in exploring the link between access to finance and firms' performance, the results obtained are still unclear and inconclusive. Moreover, very little work has been done on access to finance and manufacturing SMEs performance especially in developing countries context (Abegaz, 2013). The purpose of this study is to fill this literature gap by examining the dual effects of access to bank credit on SME performance in line with productivity and profitability in Ethiopia.

The research questions entail the translation of the research problem into the need for inquiry (Murthy & Bhojanna, 2008). Accordingly, the research problem defined above leads to the research questions that the present study aims to address:

1. How important is finance access to improve Small and Medium Manufacturing Enterprise productivity and profitability in Ethiopia?
2. How does access to bank credit affect productivity and profitability of Small and Medium Manufacturing Enterprises in developing countries like Ethiopia?
3. How and to what extent, can access to finance influences SME productivity and profitability performance in developing countries particularly in Ethiopia?

The book will enhance the importance of access to external finance and SME performance in terms of productivity and profitability. The study adapts different models to improve prediction and explanation of the components of finance on SMEs performance in Ethiopia. This study investigates how, and to what extent, access to finance influences SME performance. This helps to understand how the typical value of the productivity and profitability (dependent variable) of SMEs changes when one of the inputs such as access to bank credit (independent variable) is varied, while the other independent variables are fixed.

The scope of the study is limited to the registered SMEs (i.e. mixture of incorporated and unincorporated firms) in all sampled region of Ethiopia which comply with the definition (i.e. definition of SMEs) given by the Central Statistics Agency of Ethiopia. Ethiopia is chosen as the institutional context for this study in order to test the external validity of development theories. The specific objectives of the study are:

- The first specific objective of the study is to determine the role of access to bank credit to improve SME productivity and profitability in Ethiopia.
- The second objective is to test empirically the hypothesis that bank credit enhances firm productivity and profitability. More specifically, this study examines whether firms with access to bank credit have relatively higher levels of performance than the other group of firms in developing country's context particularly in Ethiopia.

Various studies (Robb and Robinson, 2012; Kerr and Nanda, 2009; Black and Strahan, 2002), have found that access to finance has a critical impact on SME productivity and profitability. Nevertheless, these researches differ about the direction of causality between access to finance and enterprise productivity and profitability. Moreover, research is generally limited to studies of large and stock market-listed firms in developed countries (Butler & Cornaggia, 2007).

Some authors (Gatti & Love, 2006; Babajid, 2012; Alfaro *et al.*, 2009; Zhenhui & Sudeshna, 2011; Olutunla & Obamuyi, 2008; Shinozaki, 2012) attribute large productivity improvements to access to credit and conclude that credit is positively and strongly associated with SME productivity and profitability. However, others (Beck & Cull, 2014; Ghani & Suri, 1999; Hanson, 2001; Malesky & Taussig, 2009; Allen *et al.,* 2012) assert that the direction of causality between access to finance and SME productivity and profitability frequently runs both ways, especially for developing economies.

Moreover, the understanding of the role of access to finance on the degree and pace of change of SMEs, and the channels through which finance influences productivity and profitability, are yet to be fully grasped. Therefore, the nature of the links between SME productivity and use of credit is inconclusive (Reyes *et al.*, 2012; Babajid, 2012). There are also no studies on the extent to which bank credit affects productivity and profitability of Ethiopian manufacturing SMEs using this data set (WB, 2015). Therefore, this study aims to fill these gaps and extend existing knowledge by assesses how, and to what extent, access to finance influences SMEs performance.

This book examines the dual effects of access to bank credit on SME productivity and profitability using evidence from Ethiopian manufacturing enterprises. According to Abegaz (2013) studies related to credit, access and SMEs performance are scant in sub-Saharan Africa (SSA hereafter) mainly due to a lack of industrial census data. Moreover, there is no significant research related to access to credit and SME performance conducted in Ethiopia, especially using the manufacture survey data (WB, 2015). This objective is to fill the gap and design and use a combination of descriptive and explanatory ways in which a sample of 1,542 Ethiopian SMEs is analysed using both descriptive and inferential statistics. Descriptive statistical techniques are applied to describe characteristics of SMEs and credit access. Inferential statistical techniques, such as fixed effect analysis, are employed to measure the association of inputs to SME outputs and profit.

CHAPTER 2: ETHIOPIAN SMES CASE STUDY

2.1 INTRODUCTION

An overview of Ethiopia's economy and the performance of Ethiopian small and medium enterprises (SMEs) to provide the Ethiopian economic background, with special focus on manufacturing sector is the focus. An analysis is undertaken on the structure of business and the development of SMEs, identifying gaps in access to credit for SMEs in Ethiopia compared to the access of credit for SMEs worldwide. The selection (Ethiopia as a research context) followed the suggestion of Thong (1999) who stated that there are many differences between developing countries like Ethiopia and developed countries.

2.2 BACKGROUND

2.2.1 ECONOMIC GROWTH AND PROGRESS

According to World Bank (2015) annual report on Ethiopia's economic growth performance, over the past decade, it has achieved better economic growth compared with other low-income countries, for example, real GDP grew by 10.3 percent in 2014. Between 2000 and 2011, poverty declined from 44 to 30 percent, while income inequality remained unchanged at one of the lowest levels observed worldwide (Moller & Wacker,

2015). Over the same period, life expectancy increased from 52 to 63 years, fertility declined from seven to four children per woman, and the share of the population without education fell from 70 percent to 50 percent. Since 2000, the country moved up from being the second to the ninth poorest country in the world, according to gross national income (GNI) per capita (ibid).

Despite signs of economic growth in Ethiopia there is a fundamental question remain. What changes or adjustments are needed to address more forcefully the challenge of making Ethiopia's growth more inclusive and supportive of accelerated human development as well as to make the development sustainable? In this area, some argue that Ethiopia's economic growth has not been accompanied by transformations that translate into sustained poverty reduction and improvement in living conditions (UNDP, 2014).

Despite signs of economic growth in Ethiopia, some researchers (e. g Birara 2010 p.7) goes one step further to argue that the developmental status in Ethiopia was not designed to advance equitable growth and development throughout the country. It was designed to serve the ethnically based ruling class. To reinforce his argument Batu (2016), states that close to 70 percent of the urban dwellers of Ethiopia live in slum-like conditions. This is because; Ethiopia's current economic growth has not been accompanied by transformations that translate into sustained poverty reduction and improvement in living conditions of all citizens.

According to UNEP (2014) report, Ethiopia's slight structural change has emerged due to the growth in services sector, rather than the growth that was expected in the industry. Given the relative size of each sector, expansion of services and agriculture explain most of the GDP growth, with 4.5 percentages for the services sector and 3.1 percentages for the agriculture sector, while the contribution of industry is relatively modest at 2.1 percentages.

However, manufacturing sector, added just 0.4 percentage points to the overall growth rate of 9.7 percent in 2014 (WBG, 2015). The country's manufacturing sector is still characterised by inefficiencies and low productivity, its competitiveness in the international market is very low and its contribution to export earnings is weak (Desta, 2010b). Reasons for the lower productivity and inefficiency of the manufacturing sector could be the use of old production techniques (lack of adoption of new technologies), relative smallness of the manufacturing sector, lack of competition, shortage of supply of raw materials, lack of capital, and absence of demand (Balcha, *et al.*, 2014). According to the CSA's (2011) manufacturing survey report, 34.6 percent of firms reported shortage of raw materials as their primary reason for not operating at full capacity followed by absence of market demand, reported by 10 percent of the firms. Therefore, to sustain rapid economic growth of Ethiopia, the country should give priority to development of the manufacturing sector.

2.2.2 GEOGRAPHICAL LOCATION

Ethiopia is located in the Horn of Africa. It is situated at 3 degrees and 14.8-degree latitude, 33 degrees and 48-degree longitude in the Eastern part of Africa lying between the Equator and the Tropic of Cancer. It is bordered by Eritrea to the north, Djibouti and Somalia to the east, Sudan and South Sudan to the west, and Kenya to the south.

According to 2014 population stability report, Ethiopia is the oldest independent country in Africa. With archaeological finds dating back more than 3 million years ago. Ethiopia was a place of ancient culture and civilization. Among its important sites are Lalibela and its 12th-13th century rock-cut Christian churches, and Aksum. The ruins of an ancient city with obelisks, tombs, castles and Our Lady Mary of Zion church

Ethiopia has a high central plateau that varies from 1,290 to 3,000m above sea level, with the highest mountain, Ras Dashen reaching 4,533m. The elevation is generally the highest just before the point of descent to the Great Rift Valley, which splits the plateau diagonally. A number of rivers cross the plateau, notably the Blue Nile rising from Lake Tana. The plateau gradually slopes to the lowlands of the Sudan on the west and the Somali-inhabited plains to the east (Debonnet, *et al.,* 2006).

Since 1995, Ethiopia has been divided into 10 administrative regions based on the ethnic lines. These are Tigray, Afar, Amhara, Oromia, Somali, Benishangul, Southern Peoples' State, Gambella, Harar and Addis Ababa.

2.2.3 HISTORY

Ethiopia was reunified in 1855 by Tewodros II, and it was the beginning Ethiopia's modern history. At that time, Ethiopia was initiated slow modernisation process and defended itself from an Egyptian invasion in 1874 (Marcus, 2002). Under Menelik II, Ethiopia defeated an Italian invasion in 1896 and came to be recognised as a legitimate state by European powers. A faster and progressive civilization took place under Menelik II and Haile Selassie. However, this did not deter another Italian invasion in 1935. The modern Italian army annexed Ethiopia and combined it with its other colonies to create Italian East Africa, forcing Haile Selassie to flee the country (Marcus, 2002).

A joint force of British and Ethiopian rebels managed to drive the Italians out of the country in 1941, and Haile Selassie was returned to the throne. Ethiopia and Eritrea joined a federation, but when Haile Selassie ended the federation in 1961 and made Eritrea a province of Ethiopia a war for Eritrean independence began, lasting until 1991 (Marcus, 2002).

Haile Selassie was overthrown in 1974 and the militaristic Derg Regime came to power. In 1977, Somalia invaded tried to annex the Ogaden region but was pushed back by Ethiopian, Soviet, and Cuban forces. In 1977 and 1978, the government tortured or killed hundreds of thousands of suspected enemies in the so called 'Red Terror' (Henze, 2004).

2.2.4 POLITICAL STRUCTURE

For much of the 20th century, Ethiopia was ruled by highly centralised governments. The current ruling party, the Ethiopian People's Revolutionary Democratic Front (EPRDF) has governed Ethiopia since 1991. Since taking power, the EPRDF has led an ambitious reform to initiate a transition to a more democratic system of governance and decentralise authority. This has involved developing powers and mandates first to regional states, and then to woredas, or district authorities, and kebeles, or village authorities (ADBG, 2011).

Although the formal Ethiopian state structure has been transformed from a highly centralised system to a federal and increasingly decentralised one, a number of challenges remain. The national elections in 2005 and 2010 and the largely uncontested local elections in April 2008 illustrated the fragility of the democratic transition, the dominance of the EPRDF, and the weak opposition. The May 2010 parliamentary elections resulted in a 99.6 percent voting victory for the ruling EPRDF and its allies, reducing the opposition from 174 to only two seats in the 547 members lower house (ibid).

In January 2009, the Ethiopian Parliament passed legislation to regulate civil society organisations (CSOs). While many CSOs had long argued for a new and coherent framework, the new law is restrictive in demarcating areas of operations for different types of CSOs (for example by excluding those receiving more than 10 percent of funding from external sources from many areas of activity). The government and the Development Assistance Group (DAG), comprising bilateral and multilateral donors, have agreed that the implementation of the CSO law is reviewed regularly through their joint High-Level Forum structure (Abebe, 2012).

The government of Ethiopia is structured in the form of a federal parliamentary republic, whereby the Prime Minister is the head of government. The government exercises executive power while legislative power is vested in the Parliament. The Judiciary is more or less independent of the executive and the legislature. There are nine ethnically based administrative regions and two self-governing administrations in the capital city Addis Ababa and Dire Dawa (ibid).

The House of Peoples' Representatives elect the president of Ethiopia for a six-year term. The prime minister is chosen by the parliament. The party in power following legislative elections designates the prime minister. The Council of Ministers, according to the 1995 constitution, is comprised of the Prime Minister, the Deputy Prime Ministers, various Ministers and other members as determined and approved by the House of Peoples' Representatives. Currently, it includes the 20 members of Council of Ministers (Vestal, 2010).

The Federal Parliamentary Assembly has two chambers: the Council of People's Representatives (Yehizbtewekayoch Mekir Bet) with 547 members, elected for five-year terms in single-seat constituencies. The Council of the Federation (Yefedereshn Mekir Bet) has 110 members, one for each nationality, and 1 additional representative for each one million of its population, designated by the regional councils, which they may elect themselves or through popular elections. The president and vice president of the Federal Supreme Court are recommended by the prime minister and appointed by the House of People's Representatives; for other federal judges, the prime minister submits candidates selected by the Federal Judicial Administrative Council to the House of People's Representatives for appointment (ibid).

2.2.5 POPULATION AND LABOUR FORCE

In 2014, Ethiopia had a total population of about 85 million people, growing at 2.6 percent per year, with a total surface area of 1.1 million square kilometres. It is the second most populous country in Africa next to Nigeria (CSA, 2014). About 84 percent of the population reside in rural areas, and with only 16 percent living in urban areas, the country is one of the least urbanised countries in the world. Addis Ababa, the capital city, constitutes about a quarter of the urban population of the country.

While 15 percent of the urban population lives in towns with populations more than 100,000 but less than 250,000 and 37 percent live in medium size towns with populations between 50,000 and 100,000, while 23.3 percent live in urban centres with population size of less than 50,000 (CSA, 2014). Ethiopia is an agrarian country and agriculture accounts for 41 percent of the gross domestic product (GDP), following services 45.6 percent. Industry accounts only for 13.4 percent (MoFED, 2011a).

2.2.6 ETHIOPIAN ECONOMY AND DEVELOPMENT POLICY

The Ethiopian economy has experienced strong and broad-based growth over the past decade, averaging 10.8 percent per year in 2003/04 - 2012/13 compared to the regional average of 5.3 percent (Moller & Wacker, 2015). Expansion of the services and agricultural sectors account for most of this growth while the manufacturing sector performance was relatively modest. Private consumption and public investment explain demand side growth with the latter assuming an increasingly important role in recent years. Economic growth brought with it positive trends in reducing poverty, in both urban and rural areas (WBG, 2015). While 38.7 percent of Ethiopians lived in extreme poverty in 2004-2005, five years later this was 29.6 percent, which is a decrease of 9.1 percentages as measured by the national poverty line of less than $0.6 per day (WBG, 2014).

The first pillar of the Ethiopian Growth and Transformation Policy is "fostering competitiveness and employment," which aims to support in achieving a stable macroeconomic environment; increase agricultural productivity and marketing in selected areas. It was believed to be increasing competitiveness in manufacturing and services, and supporting SME access to financial services; improving access to and quality of infrastructure; electricity; roads; water and sanitation;

and improving regional integration by enhancing involvement in regional agriculture technology generation and dissemination (MoFED, 2010).

United Nations Development Program report (UNDP, 2012) argues that Ethiopia has achieved the Millennium Development Goals (MDGs) for child mortality and water (MoFED, 2012). There has also been encouraging progress in gender parity in primary education, HIV/AIDS, and malaria. Positive results have also been achieved in universal primary education, although the MDG target may not be met (UNDP, 2014).

However, poverty continues to be a major challenge to the country's sustainable development and stability (MoFED, 2012). Research results indicate that around half of the population who are living in both urban and rural areas of the country are victims of poverty. This is due to a lack of economic opportunities, government crisis, inadequate basic household income, and poor means of survival (Mammo, 2008).

Ethiopia's economy is extremely reliant on rain-fed agriculture that constitutes 41 percent of GDP, followed by services at 45.6 percent. Industry accounts only for 13.4 percent of GDP (MoFED, 2011b). Moreover, the urban and rural population of the country in the age group between 15 to 30 years are unemployed because of lack of opportunities (Altenburg, 2010).

Since the past two decades, poverty reduction has been the core of the country development plans (ADBG, 2011). In addition to this, recently the Ethiopian government has launched another five-year plan (2011-2015), the Growth and Transformation Plan (GTP), which has been developed to maintain rapid and broad-based economic growth to end poverty towards the realisation of the MDGs (MoFED, 2010).

This plan envisages the transformation of the economy by commercialising the agricultural sector and significantly increasing the share of the manufacturing sector in GDP (ibid). With the core objective of attaining economic growth and development, this poverty reduction economic policy initiative have been undertaken by promoting the development of SMEs through privatisation policy. In other words, the role of the SME sector is highly acknowledged as a way to reduce unemployment, to enhance economic growth and reduce poverty (Bekele & Zeleke, 2008).

As a result, the issue of SME development is given high attention and explicitly stated in the country's core strategic policy plans, like the Country Poverty Reduction Strategy, Micro and Small Enterprises Development Strategy and the Federal Food Security Strategy. Despite the above poverty reduction plans at country level, giving more emphasis to SME development and vibrant private sector, until recently, and low productive firms mostly in the informal sector dominate the economy, while the highly productive SME sector can be found only in a few regions (Altenburg, 2010).

2.3 FINANCIAL SECTOR

The Ethiopian banking sector's total assets increased by more than 13 percent within a one year period from mid-2013 to mid-2014 (Wondifraw *et al.,* 2015). The majority of the total assets are owned by three public banks, which constitute 77 percent of total assets of the financial sector excluding the assets of both development and national banks, while insurance companies and Micro Finance Institutions (MFIs) represent 2.2 percent and 5.2 percent respectively of Ethiopia's financial sector assets (WBG, 2015).

Government owned banks that are mainly interested in financing large enterprises dominates the banking sector in Ethiopia. Respectively, the share of private banks in credit lending has dropped from 39 percent of the market share in 2009/10 to 32 percent in 2011/12, while that of the public banks it raised from 61 to 68 percent during the same period (Keatinge, 2014).

Market share of the biggest bank, the state owned Commercial Bank of Ethiopia (CBE), has declined over time.

The same trend holds in degree of concentration in the private commercial bank market. Despite CBE's declining share of deposits, it still accounts for about 59 percent of outstanding deposits. This might be a combined effect of its monopoly over government banking service demand and public trust considering its age (>50 years) and extensive branch network (ibid).

An expansion of credit to the private sector enables firms to invest in productive capacity thereby laying the foundation for a sustainable growth path. However, Ethiopia is falling behind its peers in this area. In 2011, credit to the private sector in Ethiopia was equivalent to about 14 percent of GDP compared to the regional average of 23 percent (WB, 2015). The share of SME lending comprises only 7 percent of bank is overall lending portfolios, which is much lower than other Sub-Saharan countries as well as far below that of developing economies (WB, 2015). Private Banks performs well in terms of profitability, scale efficiency and quality of credit, while state banks offer a lower interest rate (Bezabeh and Desta, 2014).

2.3.1 IMPERIAL PERIOD (1905 -1974)

The history of banking in Ethiopia dates back to 1905 when the first bank, Bank of Abyssinia, was established by the British-owned National Bank of Egypt. Three banks that are more private were opened in the next few decades, while Bank of Abyssinia was nationalised in 1931. Moreover, the Italian occupation in the mid-1930s introduced some Italian banks to the market (Fanta, 2012).

In 1963, a new banking law allowed for greater participation of the private sector, including foreign ownership of up to 50 percent. Accordingly by the early 1970s part foreign owned banks were among the biggest private banks, even though the state-owned Commercial Bank of Ethiopia remained dominant (Bezabeh and Desta, 2014). However, this progress was halted with the transition to socialism in 1974.

2.3.2 FINANCIAL REPRESSION (1974-1991)

Transition to a state owned economy in 1974 introduced various financial regulations that halted the development of effective financial institutions. Complete restrictions on entry meant that all private banks were nationalised and reorganised into three big state owned banks. Directed lending required all banks to lend in support of state plans. Interest rate ceilings meant that neither lending nor saving rates were determined by the market (Geda, 2006).

During this period, the Central Bank served limited purposes. For example, administering loans and exchange rate allocation as dictated by central plans, then directly financing government deficit and enforcing the interest rate ceiling. Coupled with government guarantees on loans to public enterprises, these policies are argued to have left little room for banks to engage in actual credit appraisal (ibid). According to Addison and Geda (2001), the policy environment wiped out the little commercial lending practices accumulated during the Imperial period, along the way blocking the chance to develop financial market institutions.

2.3.3 FINANCIAL REFORM (SINCE 1992/93)

With transition to a market economy in 1992/93 some of the earlier repressive policies were relaxed (Geda, 2006). Some of the restrictions maintained are control on capital flow, which means domestic agents are not allowed to borrow or lend abroad and foreign banks are not allowed to operate in the domestic economy in any form (Addison and Geda (2001). State ownership is maintained, restricting privatisation of state banks in any form. The government continues to regulate the minimum savings rate and some of the relaxed policies allowed domestic entry, whereby private banks were allowed to operate if 100 percent locally owned (Geda, 2006). There was more power in lending decisions for state banks and 100 percent autonomy for private banks. Lending rates were also deregulated, such that lending rates were determined fully by the market (Fanta, 2012).

Institutional underinvestment in financial market infrastructure from the socialist period was one of the key challenges in the early years of the reform (Geda, 2006). The only source of experience in commercial lending was the state owned Commercial Bank of Ethiopia itself with little commercial lending practice (Fanta, 2012). At the same time the new private banks, the state banks and the Supervision & Regulation Department were all competing for limited human capital in the banking system (Ashenafi, 2012). The Government's strong position for continuing state ownership and restriction on foreign participation was backed by the arguments of; maintaining equity in access to finance, capital account stability, limited regulatory capacity and the infant industry protection argument (Kiyota *et al.,* 2007).

2.3.5 TRENDS IN ENTRY VS TOTAL LOANS

National Bank of Ethiopia report showed that, the years after deregulation saw a slow but steady growth in the number of new banks. Fourteen domestic private banks had joined the market in two waves; six banks in 1994 -1999 and eight banks in 2004-2011. Six more banks are under formation currently (NBE, 2011a). However further entry is expected to be greatly undermined by the recent raise in minimum paid up capital, from 75 million to 500 million Br (566 per cent increase) (ibid).
Outstanding deposits expanded steadily but started to slow down since 2008; this may be a response to the growing inflation, which peaked at 64 percent in 2008 (Zwedu, 2014). Loans, on the other hand, grew relatively slowly but picked up in 2004 (80 percent growth rate). State bank credit expanded the most in 2004; 128 percent vs. 50 percent in private bank credit (Addison and Geda, 2001).

2.3.5 MARKET CONCENTRATION VS BANK PERFORMANCE

Market share of the biggest bank, the state owned Commercial Bank of Ethiopia, declined over time (Geda, 2006). The same trend held in degree of concentration in the private commercial bank market. The CBE's share of deposits had declined relatively slowly, however it still accounts for about 59 percent of outstanding deposits. This might be a combined effect of its monopoly over government banking service demand, public trust considering its old age (>50 years) and its wide branch network (ibid).

2.3.6 EVIDENCE OF IDLE RESOURCE: EXCESS RESERVE

Excess reserve and liquidity were serious between 2002 and 2004. However, both started to decline since 2004, the year when lending started to expand faster. On average, state banks were not the major source of excess liquidity as is usually believed based on the assumption that state banks are always less efficient. Rather, every year the highest level of excess liquidity derived from the newest bank, except in 2003 and 2004 where Commercial Bank of Ethiopia had the highest level of excess liquidity (NBE, 2011).

Trade is by far the biggest recipient of bank credit from both state and private banks; on average 67 percent of private bank credit and 37 percent of state bank credit between 1999 and 2010 (NBE, 2011). Accordingly, short-term trade credits are the major loan products of Ethiopian banks (ibid).

Between 1999 and 2010, trade was the second largest sub-sector next to agriculture in terms of contribution to GDP. Moreover, it had the fastest growth rate in value-added since 2004/05 compared to agriculture and industry. Low levels of risk in trade relative to agriculture and manufacturing might be an additional reason (ibid).

A comparison of productivity of bank credit recipient enterprises in trade versus agriculture and industry would have been a more direct way to investigate why banks lend more to trade activities. However, for the lack of appropriate data on enterprises in the trade sector, the analysis searches for similar evidence in the manufacturing sector by comparing efficiency across loan recipient and non-recipient enterprises (NBE, 2011).

2.4 MANUFACTURING SECTOR

According to Kahsay (2013), the manufacturing sector is often seen as a vehicle for diversifying the economy and attaining sustainable economic growth in both developed and developing economies. However, most Sub-Saharan African economies are too dependent on agriculture and natural resource extraction (Collier, 2008). For example, Ethiopia is one of the least industrially developed countries in Sub-Saharan Africa, where the manufacturing sector accounts for only 5 percent of total value-added, while agriculture employs 85 percent of the workforce (Gebreeyesus, 2008).

According to the World Bank (2014a) enterprises survey data, many countries in Sub-Saharan Africa report a high number of SMEs in the economy. However, the contribution of the sector is insignificant to countries economy (Abegaz, 2013). Various factors contribute to this phenomenon, including the lack of access to finance, lack of basic infrastructure, inadequate private and public investment, and the lack of consistent public policy aimed at promoting industrial development World Bank (2014b). The following table illustrates industrial performance in Ethiopia and sub-Saharan African (SSA) countries generally.

Table 2.1: Industrial Performance Indicators for Ethiopia and SSA 2005-2008

Year	% Share of MFG in total value-added		% Share of industry in total value-added		Manufactured exports per capita (USD)	
	Ethiopia	SSA	Ethiopia	SSA	Ethiopia	SSA
2005	0.05	0.13	0.13	0.31	0.6	62
2006	0.05	0.13	0.13	0.32	0.7	87.1
2007	0.05	0.15	0.13	0.33	2.3	110.6

2008	0.05	0.15	0.13	0.33	1.7	131.5
Average annual growth rates						
05-08	-2.3%	0.0%	1.0%	1.6%	10.7%	15.0%

Source: African Development Indicator (World Bank, 2011).

Note: a/ SSA = sub-Saharan Africa excluding South Africa and Nigeria.

Table 2.1 summarises basic economic and industrial performance indicators of SMEs over 2005-2008 for Ethiopia and for SSA. The first column indicates that per capita income has grown rapidly both in Ethiopia and SSA, however, the value share of manufacturing in total value-added has been constant over the whole period, both for SSA and for Ethiopia. This shows that there is no improvement in the manufacturing sector. Nevertheless, the overall economic growth has been relatively high and manufacturing has retained a constant share in GDP. It follows that there has been significant growth in manufacturing in absolute, although not in relative, terms. The industrial sector, defined as manufacturing plus mining, construction, electricity, water, and gas, has grown in relative importance over the period ((Demeke *et al.*, 2006).

Moreover, between 2005 and 2008, the share of industry in total GDP rose from 0.31 to 0.33 for SSA; however, for Ethiopia the value is constant. The trends for the value of manufactured exports have also grown, although for Ethiopia, this growth is an extremely insignificant. On the other side, the share of manufacturing sector in total value-added has been constant over the last half decade implies that manufacturing output has grown at the same rate as the rest of the economy for both Ethiopia and for SSA (Abegaz, 2013).

Figure 2.2 indicates wide productivity differences between Ethiopia and some SSA countries, such as Uganda and Mozambique. Not only is the productivity growth in Ethiopia much slower than in these countries, but also much more volatile. The graph shows that in 2008 enterprise productivity levels for Ethiopia were much lower than those African countries. In 2008 productivity levels for Ethiopia were 391.7, while it was 807.7 for Mozambique, and 879.3 for Uganda.

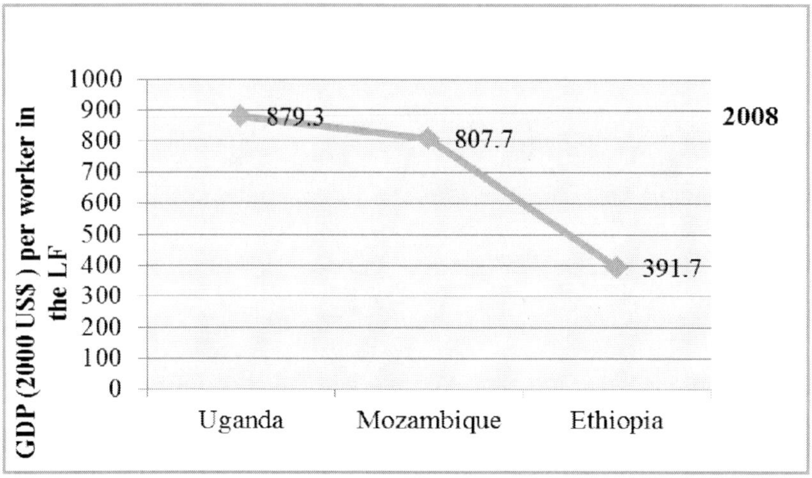

Figure 2.2: Productivity levels in Ethiopia and selected African LICs, 2008
Source: World Forum, World Bank and African Development Bank (2009)

As discussed above, in Ethiopia the manufacturing sector has a limited contribution to the overall economy of the country. The sector has been left behind and it is unable to follow other sectors of the economy, specifically agriculture and services sectors (Fanta, 2012). Dependence on light industries, low productivity, inefficiency, and lack of finance are some of the problems which limit the contribution of the sector to employment, production, and export earnings (ibid). Table 2.2 summarises sectoral contribution to GDP in Ethiopia.

Table 2.2: Sectorial Contribution to GDP and GDP Growth (in Million Birr)

Items	Sectors	Fiscal Year				
		2007/08	2008/09	2009/10	2010/11	2011/12
% Share in GDP	Agriculture	49.1	47.5	46.2	45.2	43.7

Industry	10.2	10.2	10.2	10.5	11.0
Services	41.3	42.8	43.8	44.2	45.3

Source: Ministry of Finance and Economic Development (MoFED, 2014)

Note: Sectorial contributions do not add-up to overall GDP growth because of Financial Intermediary Service Indirect Measurement (FISIM).

Table 2.2 indicates that the share of industry in GDP has remained very low with marginal to 11 percent in 2011/12 from 10.5 percent in the previous year. It shows that the manufacturing sector in Ethiopia is still at its infancy. In 2009, the industry shares of GDP value-added was 10.7 percent while that of manufacturing was 4 percent (WB, 2011). The result further confirms that the contribution of the manufacturing sector in Ethiopia is still insignificant and unsatisfactory. The economic growth is mainly driven by services and agriculture sector on the supply side (Abegaz, 2013).

Moreover, Table 2.2 shows the share of industry in GDP has remained modest, increasing to 11 percent in 2011/12 from 10.5 percent the previous year and, according to the Ministry of Finance and Economic Development (MoFED, 2014)? its growth rate averaged 14.3 percent during the years 2010-2012. The modest share and growth of the industry sector and the significant share of agriculture (44 percent) and services (45 percent) sectors clearly indicate the challenges and the needs for further structural transformation of the Ethiopian economy for the country to be able to join the category of middle-income countries within the planned period.

The contribution of the manufacturing sector in Ethiopia has limited improvement in terms of productivity, employment and exports when compared with the agriculture and services sectors of the country (Abegaz, 2013). For example, in 2009 the share of manufacturing sector to the counties of GDP value-added was 4 percent while that of the industry was 10.7 percent (World Bank, 2011). Figure 2.3 indicates the performance of Ethiopian SMEs in the manufacturing sector with respect to labour productivity.

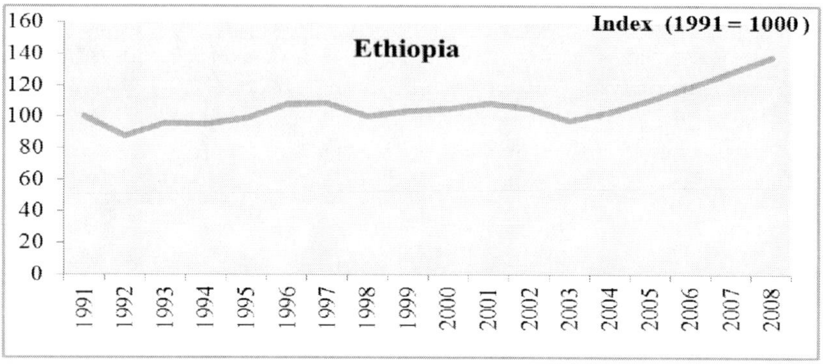

Figure 2.3: Labour Productivity, 1991 – 2008
Source: CSA'S (2011) LMMI survey 1991-2008 result.

Ethiopian manufacturing enterprises labour productivity, measured in terms of number of people employed, shows some interesting results. In Ethiopia, even if the average labour productivity increased significantly after 2003, the growth trend is still much slower and more volatile (CSA, 2011). According to the survey results of medium and large manufacturing industries as presented on Figure 2.3, the labour productivity has increased from 2003 onward. Although this growth is encouraging, labour productivity in medium and large manufacturing industries is still very small.

2.5 BUSINESS SECTOR

The role of the business sector in the Ethiopian economy has evolved in several stages. When the new government embarked on market reforms in 1991, it aimed at developing a multi-business sector economy, encouraging a rapid growth of the private business sector, attracting foreign investment and reducing bureaucratic procedures (Hansson, 2004). With these aims, the structure of Ethiopian business sector has diversified, consisting of many economic sectors. The criteria of classification of the sector could be type of ownership, business size and type of industry (WB, 2003).

Type of business structure based on ownership criteria in Ethiopia includes two main sectors: domestic and foreign-owned business (Hansson, 2004). The domestic business sector is further decomposed into state and non-state owned business sectors (WB, 2003). The non-state business sector can be further categorized into private enterprises, limited liability companies, joint stock companies, collectives or co-operatives and individual households (Tirfe, 1994). The classification of business based on the size of the businesses classified into four types; micro, small, medium and large enterprises (Ageba and Amha, 2004).

Business based on the types and features of the industry can be classified into the following major industries: agriculture and forestry, fishery, mining, manufacturing, electricity, construction, trade and services, hotels, finance and banking. It is already mentioned in scope, that this study only considers small and medium businesses operating in the manufacturing sector, whereas the micro, large and enterprises outside of manufacturing sectors are beyond the scope of this study.

2.6 DEFINING SMEs

SMEs are defined in different ways associated with concepts determined by specific contexts, for example, methods of operations, nature of markets served, size of resources employed, levels of country's economic development and so on (WB, 2015). Moreover, the definition of SMEs by size and employment creation capacity varies with respect to specific economic contexts (ibid). Some definitions (e.g. Banham and He; 2009; Ward; 2006; European Commission, 2006; World Bank, 2001; kayanula *et al.*, 2000) use capital assets to define SMEs; others use labour skills and turnover, legal status and methods of production.

In Ethiopia there is no clear national level definition for SMEs (WB, 2015). The Commission for Legal Empowerment of the Poor HLCLE (2006) paper notes that, the Ministry of Trade and Industry (MoTI) uses capital investment as criteria, while the Central Statistical Agency (CSA) uses employment as a baseline to define SMEs. However, the definition used by MoTI, which uses capital investment as a benchmark, has been developed for formulating the micro, small, and medium enterprise development strategy in 1997 (HLCLE, 2006). Below are some popular definitions of SMEs used in the Ethiopian context?

2.6.1 MINISTRY OF TRADE AND INDUSTRY

Enterprises with annual turnover capital of between Birr 500,000 and Birr 1.5 million and/or enterprises with assets excluding fixed property between Birr 4 million and Birr 15 million depending on the type of industry are "medium enterprises". Those enterprises with capital between Birr 20,000 and Birr 500,000 and/or enterprises with assets excluding fixed property between Birr 1.5 million and Birr 4 million depending on the type of industry are "small enterprises" (MoTI, 2004).

2.6.2 ETHIOPIAN CENTRAL STATISTICS AGENCY

Enterprises employing 6 to 10 people and using motor-operated equipment are considered as small-scale manufacturing enterprises, and enterprises employing 50 to 99 persons, depending on the type of industry, are "medium enterprises" (CSA, 2004).

2.6.3 WORLD BANK

The definitions used by the World Bank in the Ethiopian context uniformly use the number of employees' criteria. Enterprises with 10 to 20 employees are considered as small enterprises and enterprises with 21-99 employees are categorised as medium enterprises. Table 2.3 gives summarised definitions of SMEs.

Table 2.3 Summarised definitions of SMEs

Country Name	Year	MSME Definitions (number of employees, otherwise noted)	
		Small	**Medium**
South Africa	2004	<50; turnover<R 32mil (differentiated by sector)	Agri <100; other <200; turnover <R64mil(differentiated by sector)
Kenya	2006	11-50	51-100
Brazil	2007	10-49	50-249
India	2007	Mfg.: Invst < US$ 1 mil, Servc.: Invst. < US$ 0.4 mil	Mfg.: Invst. < US$ 2 mil, Servc: Invst. < US$ 1 mil
China	2009	<300 Indstr, <600 Constr.	<2000 Indstr, <3000 Constr.
	2006	<100 Wholesale, <100 Retail	<200 Wholesale, <500 Retail
US		<500 Transp, <400 Post <400 in Hotels & Restaurants	<3000 Transp, <1000 Post <800 in Hotels & Restaurants
		10-99	100-499
EU		11-50	51-100
Ethiopia	2004	10-20	21-100

Source: Kushnir *et al.,* (2010) & WB Enterprises survey of Ethiopia (2011b)

The various SME's definitions across the world show it is difficult to find a single universal definition of SMEs. Different countries and institutions use different criteria to define and measure SMEs e.g. annual sales or turnover and/ or number of employees, and to tailor the specific size breakdown to particular conditions in the country of operation.

2.6.4 SME POLICY

At present, the Ethiopian government is aware of the positive contribution SMEs. Government has realised that SMEs can play major role in Ethiopia economy development. After the current government took power in 1991, different economic policy initiatives have been undertaken to promote the development of SMEs through privatisation policies, with the objective of attaining economic growth (Bekele & Zeleke, 2008). The role of the SME sector is acknowledged in employment creation, economic growth and poverty alleviation. The country's core strategic policies, such as the five-year Growth and Transformation Plan (GTP), Micro and Small Enterprises Development Strategy plan and the Federal Food Security Strategy, place focus on the expansion and strengthening of SMEs (MoUDC, 2013). Different strategies, such as the Federal Micro and Small Enterprise Development Strategy (FMSDS) and Regional Micro and Small Enterprise Development Strategy (RMSDS) are designed to create a suitable environment for the development of SMEs in Ethiopia (MoFED, 2003). Many other related laws have been passed to create a proper environment for the development of SMEs.

Enterprise development and promotion efforts in Ethiopia started in the late 1950s. As a result, several policy reforms related to development and promotion of SMEs were undertaken at different stages and under different regimes. Some of the strategy and policy proclamation reforms are:

- *Business Enterprises Registration Proclamation No. 184/1961.* The main objective of this proclamation was to register business enterprises under the Ministry of Commerce and Industry.
- *Investment Proclamation No. 242/1966.* The objective of this strategy was to provide SME tax relief, access to land, building, public utilities and other advisory and administrative services. During this period, enterprise promotion efforts in Ethiopia had traditionally focused on urban-based SMEs (Degefe, 1986).
- *Industrial Regulation Legal Notice No. 292/1971.* The aim was to provide enterprise temporary licenses

The Ministry of Industry and Tourism was responsible for coordinating promotional activities which includes provision of training on business management. The Socialist era of 1974 1991 was characterised by nationalisation of firms throughout the country by Proclamation No 26/1975.

The Economic policy of the socialist regime was based on central planning system. Private property was nationalised and private sector activities were discouraged. In the socialist regime few services and producers' cooperatives enterprises were formed, their numbers increased and then decreased through bankruptcy, lack of imported inputs. Eventually at that time private investment in the sector was virtually ceased (UNDP, 2012).

New government embarked on market reforms in 1991, aimed at reducing bureaucratic procedures and encouraged rapid growth of the private sector and enterprises (MoFED, 2011). Together with several other supporting proclamations, the current regime launched market economy development, public and private sector reform (Assefa *et al.,* 2014). The Plan for Accelerated and Sustained Development to End Poverty (2005-2010) identified SMEs as a foundation and catalyst for the economy, for job creation and to reduce poverty ibid).

The current country development strategy is Growth and Transformation Program (2010-2015) also gives priority to SME development. The program is situating SME development as one of the seven identified growth pillars of the county (MoFED, 2010). The Government of Ethiopia has revisited the whole issue of SME promotion but with more focus on Micro and Small Enterprises (MoFED, 2011).

The respective Micro and Small Enterprises strategies help to augment contributions of SMEs, Medium and Large-scale industries (Assefa *et al.,* 2014). Even if most of the reviewed development policies are designed towards promotion of SMEs, the link between the expansion of medium and large enterprises is not clear in terms of access to resources (MoFED, 2010). Although recent progress should not be underestimated,

Ethiopia's SME sector is still in its infancy and many challenges remain such as unfavourable legal and regulatory environments and, in some cases, discriminatory regulatory practices (ibid).

2.7 SME CHALLENGES

SMEs in Ethiopia are faced with many problems irrespective of their process of development. These include shortage of capital, technology, policy challenges, structural challenges, institutional challenges and bottlenecks. Some of these challenges are internal while others are external to the enterprise (WB, 2014b). The most common challenges that hinder SMEs efficiency and effectiveness are lack of access to finance, lack of training in managerial and entrepreneurial skills, poor infrastructure, and social and cultural factors like extensive corruption, deficient entrepreneurial culture, and government over-regulation (Ebashi *et al.*, 1997; WB, 2014b). Ministry of Urban Development and Construction (MoUDC, 2013) survey results, observed that, SME owners in selected Ethiopian cities complained about the lack of finance to expand their business (42 percent), a lack of access to working premises (28.3 percent); and lack of access to markets.

2.8 SME FINANCING

SMEs play a crucial role in economic growth, innovation and prosperity. However, most Ethiopian SMEs operate in the informal sector, which is characterised by low production and productivity, low levels of competition (AfDB, 2011). Bigsten & Gebreeyesus (2007) stated that the SME sector has performed poorly in terms of output, employment generation, and entry into the global market." The main reason for poor performance of SMEs in Ethiopia is that the sector is constrained by weaknesses in the finance sector due to perceived and actual risks (high administrative costs, high collateral requirements and lack of experience with financial intermediaries).

Ethiopia's financial sector is inefficient since it is small, fragmented and lacks depth. Due to these and other reasons, the sector is unable to offer satisfactory services on the scale required. This is a major obstacle to the expansion of businesses, especially for SMEs, and development of export capacity (AfDB, 2011). Ethiopia lags behind other sub-Saharan African countries and developing countries in terms of lending to SMEs (WB, 2015). The share of SME lending comprises only 7 percent of overall bank lending, which is significantly lower than other Sub-Saharan African countries and far below that of other developing economies (WB, 2015).

Enterprises may use internal and/or external sources of finance. Internal sources of finance include owner's capital and retained earnings, while external sources of enterprise finance include borrowing from formal and informal sources, implicit borrowing in the form of accounts payable, hire purchase, and lease-to-buy contracts (Gebrehiwot & Wolday, 2006). In Ethiopia most potential sources of finance for SMEs are friends/relatives, credit suppliers', and Iqub (rotating savings and credit associations), conventional banks, microfinance institutions, cooperatives and government projects (Kuntchev *et al.,* 2012).

In developing countries, particularly in Ethiopia, SMEs cannot access primary and secondary money and capital markets, because such markets do not exist either altogether or enterprises are not in a position to access such markets for several reasons (Nichter and Goldmark, 2009). For instance, raising funds through securities (bond and equity) involves listing requirements that are too stringent and costly for many firms to meet. Gebrehiwot and Wolday (2006) reveal that friends/relatives are the most frequently used sources of financing, followed by supplier credit, Iqub and banks.

According to Worku (2013), the majority of SMEs in Ethiopia are without access to credit from formal financial institutions such as commercial banks. However, Iqub schemes can be viewed as a form of social capital in which participants generate financial and non-financial benefits such as interest-free loans, savings, the exchange of productive information and vital knowledge, skills and innovative ideas (ibid).

SMEs use loans most commonly for the purchase of inputs/raw materials and working machinery regardless of the source of finance. Except saving and credit associations, SME credit providers, formal and informal, normally provide short-term loans for less than a year (MoUDC, 2013).

World Bank (2011b) enterprises survey data shows that, lack of access to external finance for enterprises is identified as the major factor for the low productivity performance of enterprises in Ethiopia. Enterprises rely excessively on internal finance for their business operations. This supports the argument that inefficient financial markets increase the reliance on the internal source of finance.

Survey results presented in Figure 2.4 shows that, 86.3 percent of small firm's operation costs are covered by internal sources of finance. Only 8.2 percent of the finance source was from bank credit (WB, 2011b). It implies that the vast majority of small firms did not have access to bank credit. This appears to agree with the idea that enterprises that lack access to bank credit rely on internal sources as a substitute (Worku, 2013). In general, the chart below shows that there is an excessive reliance on internal funds by small and medium enterprises and it is a sign of potentially inefficient financial intermediation in Ethiopia.

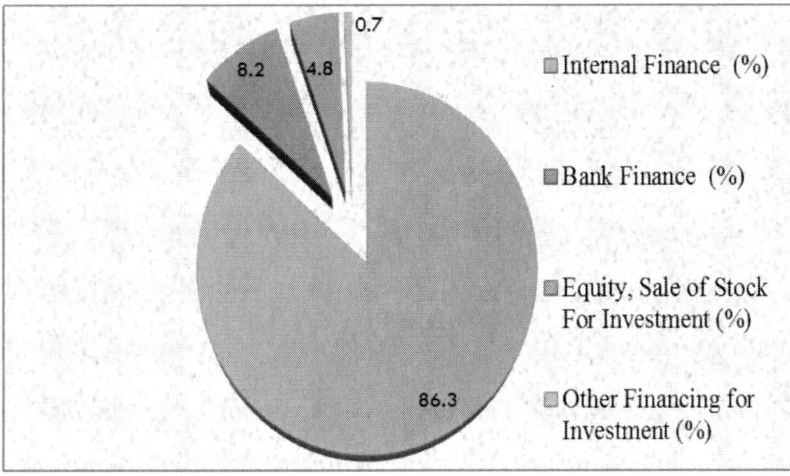

Figure 2.4: Sources of Finance and percent of SMEs reporting them as primary

Source: World Bank Enterprises Survey Data (2011b) report

2.9 CONCLUSION

Ethiopia is undergoing transition from socialist economy to a market-oriented economy and has achieved remarkable economic growth in recent years (Moller & Wacker, 2015; WBG, 2015; MoFED, 2010). Despite this progress, more effort is required for further economic transformation, to meet the population's basic needs and to create sustainable improvement in living conditions of citizens by means of poverty reduction. In order to achieve the current economic growth, the government of Ethiopia adopted different strategic policy reforms at different levels. Based on these policy reforms, SMEs in Ethiopia have opportunities to develop and create employment. However, SMEs have many challenges in the process of development.

Financing is one of the most difficult issues faced by SMEs (Ebashi *et al.*, 1997) SMEs cannot easily obtain bank credit for establishment and expansion. This leads SMEs to use internal and informal source of financing as a major means of fund and use short-term loans to finance non-current assets (Worku,

2013). Moreover, different rules for different banks and periodic changes in rules lead to negative impacts on financial policy for SMEs (Keatinge, 2014). As a result, SMEs often maintain relatively high current ratios to respond to the regularly changing business conditions. Prevailing bank credit facilities and operation in an uncertain business environment has adversely affected SME productivity and profitability (Wondifraw *et al.,* 2015).

The next chapter (chapter 3) deals with the theoretical foundations of the research related theories, review of previous studies on access to finance, SME productivity and profitability in both developed and developing economies, presents conceptual frameworks for the research and defines commonly used concepts in the research.

CHAPTER 3: THE THEORIES TO CREATE THE RELEVANT BODY KNOWLEDGE

3.1 INTRODUCTION

In general, a literature review helps to demonstrate familiarity with the body of knowledge and establishes credibility, as well as shows how the current research project is linked to past research (Neuman, 2006). Moreover, the literature review helps to integrate and summaries what is known in an area of the study, and stimulates new ideas (ibid). In addition, the literature review shows what research has been done in the field, the research methods used, the results generated and what was done with the findings (du Plooy, 2009). Therefore, all empirical studies must be connected to literature to support the need for the study and situate it in terms of previous work (Rocco & Plakhotnik, 2009:120).

Accordingly, this chapter is a review of the literature on the link between access to bank credit and SME performance around the world. It begins with a discussion on related financial and economic growth theories that explains the importance of SMEs' financing which may aid in the understanding of financing and SMEs' performance. Respectively, the next section identifies the role of financing with respect to theories.

It highlights the definitions of each theory and postulates that helps to discuss the study objective in detailed. At the last, this chapter presents review of the previous studies relating finance access, SMEs productivity and profitability performance. The final section identifies the gaps in the literature, articulates the gaps and finds the possible directions of this research.

3.2 FINANCING AND RELATED THEORIES

The significance of theory is "theory organises and refines our ideas, like a map for exploring unexplored territories" (Stacks & Salwen, 2009:4). In this view, this study is multidisciplinary in nature because it combines theories and policies from diverse but related fields of finance, productivity, profitability, and growth. The theory section of the thesis is organised as follows: firstly, it presents and discusses the SME finance related theories and its applications. Secondly it discusses SME productivity and profitability related theories and its applications. Finally, it argues important terms and concepts specific to finance, firm productivity and profitability performance.

3.2.1 PECKING ORDER THEORY

The pecking order theory initially established and discussed by Donaldson (1961), who found that owner-managers prefer to finance investment using retained earnings instead of external funds like bank credit, regardless of the size of the firm. The theory was further simplified by Myers and Majluf (1984) where they argue that equity is a less chosen means to raise capital. When managers (who are expected to know better about true situation of the firm than stockholders) issue new equity, stockholders consider that the firm is overvalued and managers are taking advantage of this over-valuation (Myers, 1977). As a result, investors will place a lower value to the new equity.

The theory further affirms that following particular financing hierarchy will maximise the value of the firms (Myers and Majluf, 1984; Myers, 1977, Myers, 1984). The basic assumptions of the theory are no optimal credit-to-equity ratio. The theory also categorizes financing sources into three major groups, *internal funds, credit and new equity* (Myers and Majluf, 1984). Companies prioritize their sources of financing, first choosing internal source of financing, and then credit/debt, lastly raising equity as a last option or "last resort" (Ou and Haynes, 2006).

Hence, the first priority is to use internal financing; when that is exhaustedly used, then credit or debt is issued; and when it is no more visible to acquire surplus credit then, equity is issued. Firms will utilise all available internal funds before looking to an external finance, especially external equities, in order to avoid dilution of control of the firm (Holmes and Kent, 1991). However, in reality, some companies issue equity even when other sources are not fully exhausted (Baker and Wurgler, 2002).

Moreover, the pecking order theory explains the transposed relationship between firm's profitability and credit/debt ratios (Hutchinson, 2003). The theory illustrates that plants choose internal financing and adapt their goal to discover their investment alternatives, while targeting to minimize unexpected deviations in dividends (Cowling *et al.,* 2012). Adhesive dividend policies, plus unexpected variations in profits and investment chances, implies that internally produced cash flow is more than capital expenses and at other times less (sentence not clear) (Hutchinson, 2003).

If external financing is required, firms issue the safest security first (Lopez-Gracia and Sanchez-Andujar, 2007). That is, they always start with credit/debt, and then shift to possible safe alternatives such as convertible bonds, then possibly equity as a last resort (ibid). Moreover, cost incurred is relatively small for internal funds, followed by debt and highest for equity. There is also side effect to the stock market associated with issuing equity, positive signalling associated with debt (Newman *et al.*, 2011).

In general, this theory illustrates that any investment or business follow to a certain steps of financing sources and prefer internal financing when it is accessible, and credit is preferred over equity if there is a need for external financing (equity is by definition issuing shares which meant 'bringing external ownership' into the company). Thus, the form of credit a firm select can act as an indication of its need for external finance (Scott, 1976).

3.2.2 TRADE-OFF THEORY

The trade-off theory was initially formulated and discussed by Myers and Majluf, (1984), who refers capital structure to the idea that an organization picks the level of debt finance and how much equity finance to use by balancing the costs and benefits. This theory often sets up as a competitor theory to the pecking order theory of capital structure developed by (Myers, 1984).

The classical version of the theory's argument and hypothesis goes back to Frank and Goyal (2005) who considered a balance among the dead-weight costs of insolvency and the tax saving benefits of credit/debt. Miller (1998) for instance evaluated this balancing as analogous to the balance between horse and rabbit content in a stew of one horse and one rabbit. Taxes are large and they are sure, while bankruptcy is rare and, according to Miller, it has low dead-weight costs'. Accordingly, the above author proposed that if the trade-off theory were true, then firms ought to have much higher credit/debt levels than we observed in reality (Eriotis and Ventoura, 2007).

In addition, Fischer, Heinkel, and Zechner (1989) popularise a dynamic trade-off theory. This theory stresses the deviating debt ratio from the target, in a situation where the costs of adjusting the debt ratio are higher than the costs of maintaining sub-optimal capital structure. According to this theory, there is a negative association between profitability and leverage, since firms reflexively accumulate profits and losses and let the debt ratios deviate from the target. Similarly, according to Hovakimian, *et al* (2001), firms that were highly profitable in the past are likely to have low gearing. Although, there are quite a number of studies (e.g. Bhaduri, 2002; Bancel and Mittoo, 2004; Gaud *et al.,* 2005; Beattie *et al.*, 2006) that verified that the firms manage leverage towards a target ratio, nevertheless, the evidence is indecisive.

Empirical investigations in the SMEs' literature did not find strong evidence to support trade-off theory (Sogorb-Mira, 2005). This is because SMEs face difficulties in accessing adequate debt financing in order to get tax shields in view of the fact that they are less likely to generate a tremendous amount of profit in comparison to the larger firms (Pettit and Singer, 1985) and this complements the findings of Michaelas *et al.* (1999). A similar finding was derived by Matsaganis and Flevotomou (2010), who affirmed that debt level was not affected by tax considerations. Indeed, previous work indicates that SME owner-managers tend to operate without targeting an optimal debt to equity ratio (e.g. Holmes and Kent, 1991).

3.2.3 LIFE CYCLE THEORY

The 'financial life cycle' or sometimes called 'growth cycle theory' originates from economics literature (Penrose, 1952; Timmons, 2004) and the theory is normally used to describe the development of the firm based on its consumption and saving behaviour or through its growth phases. In addition, life cycle model explained the development of financing needs and capital structure of the firm (Timmons, 2004). This theory is relevant to SMEs as they are dense and carry high information costs (Psillaki and Daskalakis, 2009), especially those with a relatively short historical performance.

The life cycle theory for small and medium size enterprises (SMEs) patented and developed by Berger and Udell (1998). It postulates that financial needs and available financing options of SMEs change as firms become big, matured, old, and more translucent and organized informationally. Berger and Udell (1998) use data from several US datasets to explain how firm's financing changes over time. They demonstrate that financing choices and needs change as a firm grows in size, gains more experience and becomes more transparent. However, Gregory *et al.* (2005) evaluated this theory and argued that it is not possible to encompass the life-cycle of SMEs in one model, as implied by Berger and Udell (1998).

This is because the model is unable to present a full scenario with reference to the relationship between firm characteristics and capital structure. However, there are quite a number of previous studies (e.g. Petersen and Schuman, 1987; Fluck, Holtz-Eakin, and Rosen, 1998; Mac a Bhaird and Lucey, 2006) in line with the applicability of the life-cycle model in explaining the financing decisions of SMEs.

According to Petersen and Schuman, (1987) the theory predicts that the firm in its early stage of development relies significantly on internal finance. As the firm develops, it is able to obtain more external finance because outsiders are able to scrutinise its creditworthiness. That means if a firm grows, it will attract venture capital as a source of intermediate equity, and mid-term loans for intermediate debt; finally, as it is more informationally transparent, it will acquire access to public equity or long-term debt (Fluck, Holtz-Eakin, and Rosen, 1998; Mac a Bhaird and Lucey, 2006). However, firms will use less debt in the later stages of development since they use to retained profits to financial investment.

3.2.4 PIKETTY AND MARGINAL PRODUCTIVITY THEORY

This theory used to analyse the profit-maximizing quantity of inputs that is, the services of factor of productions purchased by a firm in the production of output (Moseley, 2012a). This theory explains that the demand for a production inputs is based on the additional units gain from factors of inputs (Moseley, 2012b). A firm is generally ready to pay a better price for an input that is more productive and contributes more to output. The demand for a production input is thus best named as a derived demand.

Marginal productivity theory is a foundation in the analysis of factor markets and the input side of short-run production (Biewen & Weiser, 2011). It provides good understanding into the demand for factors of production based on the notion that a profit-maximizing firm hires inputs based on a comparison between the productivity of the input and the cost of the input (ibid).

Firm's productivity is termed as an average measure of the efficiency of production and it can be estimated as the ratio of output to inputs used in the production process, i.e. output per unit of input (Ross *et al.,* 1999). In economics, the value of outputs minus the value of inputs gives a measure of the income generated in a production process. It is a measure of total efficiency of a production process and the objective is to be maximized in production process (Syverson, 2011).

According to Biesebroeck (2008), firms' partial productivity can be estimated based on one or more inputs or factors of production, but not all factors. A common example in economics is labor productivity, usually expressed as output per hour. At the company level, typical partial productivity measures are; worker hours, materials or energy per unit of production (Bartelsman & Mark, 2000). Moreover, in the production process output is obtained by summing up the value-added created in the single process (Beveren, 2010). This is done in order to avoid the double counting of intermediate inputs and the value-added is obtained by subtracting the intermediate inputs from the outputs (ibid).

In addition, Moseley (2014) asserts that productivity is a crucial factor in production performance of firms and nations. It is also true that increasing national productivity can raise living standards because people's ability to purchase goods and services depend on the level of real income. That means if there is more real income can allow a better life for people and it also helps businesses to be more profitable (Biesebroeck, 2005).

3.2.5 FREE CASH FLOW THEORY

Free cash flow (FCF) is a measure of financial reform calculated as operating cash flow minus capital expenditure (Brigham and Ehrhardt, 2013). It represents the cash that a company is able to generate after laying out the money required to maintain or expand its asset base (Paul and Raith, 2001). Free cash flow is important because it allows a company to pursue opportunities that enhance shareholder value (Aydogan, 2003). Without cash, it's tough to develop new products, make acquisition pay dividends and reduce debt (Almeida *et al.*, 2004).

According to George and Mozumdar (2001) free cash flow is the excess of cash required that could be used for maintaining asset base, or funding and expanding projects. On the other side the notion and concept of free cash, states that managers with large amounts of free cash flow prefer to undertake non-optimal activities (Fazzari, 2000).

When the operating cash flow of the organisation is more than its profitable investment opportunities, high-debt levels will increase the value of the firm. Moreover, when the organisation generates substantial free cash flow, conflicts of interest between shareholders and managers over pay off policies are severe (Kaplan and Zingales, 2000). Too much cash may encourage managers to take it easy, and expand their benefits with cash that should be paid back to shareholders. Another problem is to motivate managers to utilise the cash instead of investing it below the cost of capital.

Normally managers tend to allocate the firm's resources to their private benefit, especially when the firm is mainly equity financed (Jensen and Meckling, 1976). Jensen (1986) suggested that debt can be an effective substitute for dividend since it would tie up the owner-managers to pay out the debts for future cash flow. Debt may limit management spending in such a way that the excess cash flow may spend in non-profitable investments. The excess cash flow will be used to repay debts which indirectly diminishing the management's control over the cash flows (Brigham and Ehrhardt, 2013).

3.2.5 CREDIT RATIONING THEORY

Hodgman [1960, 1962] that discussed credit rationing with the rational profit maximizing decisions point of view has initiated modern credit rationing theory. The theory is well known on financing gap analysis and Stieglitz & Weiss (1983) modify it. The main argument of the theory is that, information asymmetries are the key reason why credit-seekers, such as SMEs, have constrained access to finance.

By their very nature, financial markets are highly prone to information asymmetry, where only a firm itself knows its real financial structure, the real strength of the investment project and the effective intention to repay the debt, is firm's own private information (Deakins *et al.,* 2008). Stieglitz and Weiss (1983) also discuss credit rationing and argue that SMEs face financial resource constraints due to two important gaps. These are the information asymmetry gap and the agency problems. The financial market behaviours restrict access to finance for SMEs.

In other words, borrowers know more about their projects than lenders do, and their commitments for future repayment do not always turn out to be self-reinforcing. This phenomenon is called 'adverse selection' and 'moral hazard' (Peter & Montiel, 2003:11). To ameliorate these risks in turn entails a high cost of financial intermediation for individual agents in the form of searching, matching, screening, post-loan monitoring and contract enforcement. While financial institutions take advantage of this opportunity to specialise in the intermediary business, they benefit the economy. Hence, (or so) Start-up SMEs are more likely to be affected by information asymmetry problems.

3.3 POLICY AND ALTERNATIVE VIEW OF FINACEING

3.3.1 PUBLIC POLICY IN FINANCING

Allocating resources efficiently at the macroeconomic entails the cost reduction of intermediation, saving society's resources that would have been spent on individual intermediary efforts (WB, 2001b). There is an important role for financing of high return, high-risk investments that would not have been financed otherwise (ibid).

However, imperfections preclude financial markets from efficiently providing these services to the economy. Hence, policy can support the well functioning of financial markets through the provision of stable macroeconomic conditions supporting the required institutions/infrastructure (OECD, 2010). These include credit information systems, accounting disclosure standards, property rights, contract enforcement systems, adequate regulatory and supervisory frameworks to avoid collusive and excessive risk-taking behaviour among banks (ibid).

Nevertheless, financial policies do not always come in this form. They may be intended to achieve other purposes but at a cost of harmful restrictions (financial repression) or they may be designed with the right intentions but end up disrupting the market (Addison and Geda (2001). The policy also comes in the form of closing a gap under conditions where financial markets fail to serve a segment of the society (financial inclusion policies (ibid). The key policy question in finance, therefore, is to identify the areas where intervention pays off the most and to sequence it properly.

3.3.2 FINANCIAL REPRESSION

Financial repression refers to a set of policies that impose restrictions on the behaviour of domestic credit market participants, usually in exchange for achieving fiscal and/or industrial policy purposes (Roubini and Sala-i-Martin, 1991). It mainly works against the mechanisms through which finance is theoretically argued to serve the economy (ibid). Here are some of the elements and the ways their effects work.

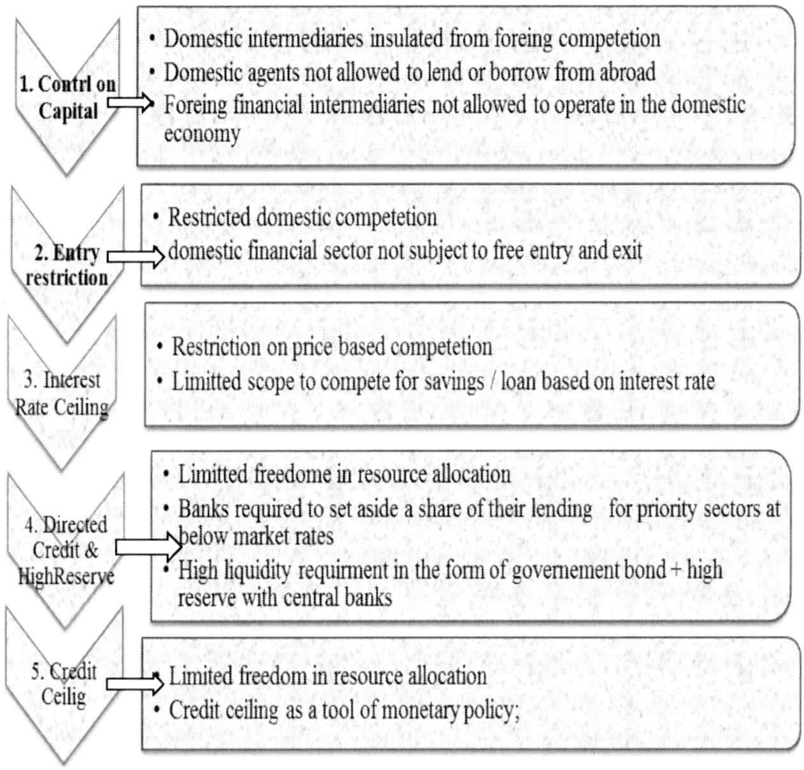

Source: Compiled from Montiel (2003, PP. 226 -236)

Although the nature of financial markets calls for government supervision and oversight, theories show that, in fact, their interaction greatly reduces the scope for better resource allocation through its effect on the behaviour of domestic economic agents (Montiel, 2003). Repressive policies tend to interact resulting in high-interest rate spreads; low returns for saving and high cost of borrowing, undermining both resource mobilisation and allocation (Dimenidas & Luintel, 1997).

A range of cross-country regressions and case studies provide evidence on the pitfalls of financial repression (Roubini & Sala-I-Martin, 1991). However, this has not been completely straightforward, for example, in East Asian case, where growth and financial repression co-existed for a considerable time (Montiel, 2003). Therefore, specific country conditions can influence the outcome of any given financial policy.

3.3.3 FINANCIAL LIBERALISATION

According to Kletzer (2004) financial liberalisation is a policy response to the adverse effects of financial repression. It implies the relaxation of all or a combination of financial restrictions. However, it does not entail a complete removal of government involvement given the inherent problem of information asymmetry in the credit market (Levine, 2001). In other words, other distortions are possible in a completely liberalised market. According to Claessens *et al.* (2009) rational bases for public policy intervention in a liberalised market are:

- *The public goods nature of information:* left alone, the market is likely to undersupply information that is a key input in the operations of financial markets.
- *The vulnerability of financial markets for systemic breakdown:* insolvency problems may lead to banking crisis, while liquidity problems may trigger bank runs.
- *Potential for financial exclusion:* the market may fail to provide financial services to a certain segment of society, especially the poor.

Lending on behalf of depositors, banks have the incentive to take excessive risk since they keep much of the upside under good outcomes and do not lose much under bad outcomes (Rajan, 2005). On the other hand, individual depositors are less likely to monitor banks, as the information that banks generate for their lending activity is costly to access.

There is a potential for free riding in monitoring and there is an implicit expectation to be bailed out by the government (Wampah, 2013). Hence, government's intervention in the form of regulation directed at avoiding adverse selection in banking prevents excessive risk taking behaviour through sound asset management supervision. Aligning the incentives of banks with depositors means ensuring that bank owners stand to bear a substantial part of the consequence in the event of insolvency (ibid).

3.4 FINANCIAL SYSTEMS AND FIRM PERFORMANCE

There are competing theories (e.g. Trade off Theory; Pecking Order Theory; Life Cycle Theory; Marginal Productivity Theory and so on) of the influence of financial systems on economic growth and firm's performance (Hoshi & Kashyap, 2004). There is a theory that financial systems positively influence economic growth by easing information and transaction costs and thereby improving the acquisition of information about resource mobilisation, financial exchange, corporate governance, and risk management (Psillaki & Daskallakis, 2009). However, some scholars (Lucas, 1988) disagree about the role of the financial sector in economic growth and firm's productivity improvement in particular. According to Lucas (1988) finance is nothing to do with economic growth or productivity improvement, but as an "over-stressed" determinant of economic growth. This perspective leads to the conclusion that, finance does not cause growth. Finance responds to changing demands from the "real sector". Another view, espoused by Miller (1998) is that, financial market development contributes to economic growth as well as firm's productivity improvement. Efficient and well-developed financial systems ease external financing constraints, which illuminate one mechanism through which financial development influences productivity improvement (Allen & Oura, 2004).

However, a growing body of empirical analyses (Allen & Oura, 2004; Tadesse, 2002; Tornell *et al.,* 2004) including firm level, industry-level studies, demonstrate a strong positive link between the functioning of the financial system and long-run economic growth (Tornell *et al.,* 2004). Moreover, microeconomic-based evidence is consistent with the idea that advanced financial systems reduce external financing constraints, which illuminates one mechanism through which financial development influences firm performance in the forms of productivity growth (Christopoulos & Tsionas, 2004). In general, theory and empirical evidence conclude that financial systems actively affect firm's productivity, profitability and growth (ibid).

This research emphasises (i) the interactions between access to finance and firm performance in terms of productivity and profitability growth. Assuming that firm's productivity growth is explained by access to finance has a greater influence on resource allocation decisions that foster firm performance rather than aggregate savings (Carlin & Mayer, 2003).

3.4.1 FIRM LIQUIDITY CONSTRAINTS

Asset liquidity is the process or mechanism with which an asset can be traded (Myers & Rajan, 1998). The more liquid an enterprise is in assets, the greater the freedom to invest beyond the limit. Enterprises with high liquid assets may be viewed as less risky by lenders. Theories suggest that more liquid assets increase firms' ability to raise cash on short notice. Some scholarly literatures suggest that the sensitivity of enterprises' investments to fluctuations in their internal funds.

According to Fazzari, (2000) most credit-constrained enterprises have investments that are more sensitive to cash flows than those credit unconstrained enterprises. However, in some cases excessive liquidity can reduce enterprises' capacity to raise external finance (World Bank, 2015). Nevertheless, enterprises' liquidity is clearly an aspect that external lenders judge when they make lending decisions, such that, if an enterprise has fewer liquidity constraints then enterprise profitability could be high. This concept is consistent with simple economic theory, which suggests that access to credit should lead to higher profits. This is consistent with the views of McMahon *et al.* (1993), Fuchs, (2011) that the financing decision influences upon the profitability of an enterprise, and with Keasey and Watson (1991), that the use of banks' financing by SMEs is associated with higher business performance.

3.5 PERIVIOUS RESEARCH FINDINGS ON STUDY TOPICS

3.5.1 SMES PRODUCTIVITY AND MEASURMENT

The needs for firms to generate productivity improvement are documented. SME productivity is very crucial in determining the success or failure of SMEs (Ahn, 2000; Bottazzi *et al.,* 2006; McMahon, 1995; Angelo *et al.,* 2007). A country's ability to improve its standard of living over time depends almost entirely on its ability to raise its output per worker and improve firm's productivity (Nagler & Naudé, 2014). However, Boyer *et al.,* (2008) argue that for all kind of business it might not be possible to be productive at the start up stage, since costs for business establishment may be higher than the returns.

However, when businesses mature, productivity has to be increased. Edmister (1970) suggests that productivity is the most catalysing factor for a business and therefore small firms should concentrate on it. Moreover, Barros *et al.,* (2013), Chikolwa, (2009) and Jen (1963) argued that productivity is a significant determinant of a small firm's credit risk. In addition, Ayed and Zouari, (2014), Dahmen and Rodríguez (2014) suggested that the aim of a business is not only the maximisation of output, but also the improvement of the productivity, since it is necessary for the development and survival of a business. Inefficiency of enterprise productivity performance leads to under-capitalisation problems because it leads to fewer dollars as earnings and therefore it increases dependence on external capital (Stierwald, 2010).

It is not easy to define and measure enterprise productivity and profitability, since enterprise's performance is difficult to conceptualise and measure (Ross *et al.,* 1999). However, productivity is commonly defined as the ratio between the input volume and the output volume (Bartelsman *et al.*, 2000). In other words, it measures how efficiently production inputs, like labour and capital, are being used in an economy to produce a given level of production output (Cressy, 1995; Michaelas et al., 1999; Cassar, 2004).

In classical economics, productivity is reflected as a key source of economic growth, competitiveness, it stands for explaining how much output is obtained from a given set of inputs, and it is typically expressed as an output–input ratio (Atkinson, 2013). Single-factor productivity measure units of output produced per unit of a particular input (ibid). It is used as basic statistical information for many international comparisons and country performance assessments (Schreyer *et al.,* 2015). There are different techniques of measuring enterprise productivity; however, the choice between them depends on the purpose of the productivity measurement and/or data availability (ibid).

The classical economic theory of firm productivity measurement goes back to the work of Tinbergen (1942) and Solow (1957). These pioneer scholars articulated firm's productivity measures in a production function context and linked them to the analysis of economic growth model. In general, following major contributions by Cobb-Douglas and Erwin-Diewert this study adopt the methods and techniques used by Tinbergen (1942) and Solow (1957) to measure SMEs productivity. Today, firm productivity measurement is well advanced and integrates to the theory of the firm, index number theory and national accounts and in general, measures of productivity growth, all of which constitute core indicators for the analysis of economic growth.

3.5.2 SMES PROFITABILITY AND MEASURMENT

In general, SMEs profitability is an abstract concept and there are many different ways to measure it. Commonly used measures of SMEs profitability are expressed at the following ratios: (1) return on sales, (2) return on assets, and (3) return on equity. In general, accounting profits are the difference between revenues and costs. However, the problem with accounting-based measures of profitability is that they ignore risk. In the economic sense, a firm is profitable only if its profitability is greater than investors can achieve independently in the capital market. However, in this study, the concept of profitability is defined and measured as a comparative model.

Firms' profitability denotes to the ratio of profit before tax and interest over sales turnover (Örtqvist *et al.,* 2006). Research shows that the profitability of a firm plays a significant role in capital structure decisions (Stierwald, 2010). According to Chakraborty (2010) a higher profitable firm tends to use internal financing and will raise credit only when additional funds are necessary. They are less likely to borrow since they can generate sufficient funding internally (Hovakimian *et al,* 2004). In general, a profitable firm could use less debt than unprofitable firms (Kemsley and Nissim, 2002). This is because the financial distress cost of debt may diminish the operation value (Phillips and Sipahioglu, 2004). Although in reality, if the more profitable firms ask for bank finance, they can easily access it and get a longer duration than less profitable firms (Riportella and Martinez, 2003) get.

Profitability has been found mainly to have an inverse impact on the debt ratio in support of pecking order theory (Zhao and Wijewardana, 2012; Usman, 2014). This implies that firms that are more profitable are more likely to choose external finance, and vice versa. This is in line with Esparanca *et al.* (2003) who discovered a negative association between profitability and debt to equity ratio. Rationally, since the owners and managers of the small firms are the same individuals, they prefer to maintain their control to their firms (Hamilton and Fox, 1998).

Thus, overinvestment is unlikely to happen. They will avoid debt (Vos *et al.,* 2007) and prefer internal financing such as retained earnings as opposed to external resources to finance in firms' activity. The following studies (see Booth et al., 2001; Ozkan, 2001; Pandy, 2001; Cassar, 2001; Fama and French, 2002; Bevan and Danbolt, 2002) on the area of small firms confirm this negative relationship between firms' profitability and debt financing.

On the other hand, trade-off theory expects a positive association between profitability and credit by considering the effect of debt tax deductibility of interest payment and low-bankruptcy risk (Ooi, 1999). Rajan and Zingales (1995) assert that debt suppliers would be reluctant to lend to less profitable firms than profitable firms would. Bhaduri (2002) also indicates a positive association between long-term debt and profitability, but a negative association with short-term borrowing. The findings of Bhaduri (2002) are relatively similar to Ozkan (2001) who shows a negative effect that is consistent with pecking-order theory.

Panno (2003) reports a negative effect, and his study reveals some evidence of positive effects consistent with the trade-off model. Hadlock and James (2002), Tong and Green (2005), Abor and Biekpe (2009), Al-Ajmi *et al.* (2009) and Ibrahim and Masron (2011) also discover a significantly positive relationship. Further, previous studies (see Myers, 1984; Myers and Majluf, 1984; Frank and Goyal, 2005; Klapper *et al.,* 2006; Abor and Biekpe, 2007; Qian *et al.,* 2009; Degryse *et al.,* 2009) also affirm that profitable firms face low cost of distress (i.e. bankruptcy) and place more value on tax deduction of interest 44 payments than less profitable firms. This situation provides incentives for profitable firms to utilise extra debt to benefit from the tax shield.

Hovakimian *et al.* (2001) discuss a different view with the dynamic trade-off theory, an inverse relationship between profitability and advantage is not because of the influence of profitability on the target advantage; rather, it affects the deviation from the target. They concluded that the negative relationship of profitability should not hold for firms that offset the deviation from the target by resetting their capital structure.

On the other hand, free cash flow theory (Jensen, 1986) expects a positive association between profitability and advantage. Debt could be a discipline device for a profitable firm (Williamson, 1988). Relatively high profitability should result in higher debt because high debt can control management discretion; this approach was used by Frydenberg (2001). Noticeably, the above rationales are expected to hold for relatively large firms. Nevertheless, this agency problem of free cash flow is non-existent in SMEs since they do not have public equity.

In addition, profitability is inversely associated with short-term debts such as trade credit (Hall *et al.,* 2000), because debt introduces an agency cost argument. Management will avoid consuming excessive perquisites and building their empires since large sums of money must be paid to creditors each year. In the case of bank financing, even though small firms can obtain loans from a commercial bank, the loan rate may be higher. Small firms may have to provide a higher premium to commercial banks in comparison with larger firms (Fu *et al,* 2002). This will lower the profitability a small firm can earn from an investment. Reliance on debt finance might also reduce the investment opportunities available for small firms. However, if less profit has been retained in the past because of lower profitability, small firms must rely more on debt financing. When a small firm relies heavily on debt as a financing source, the profitability could be lower since the debt is costly.

In relation to external equity, profitable small firms would avoid using it in order to maintain control over their firms and avoid dilution of ownership (Deesomsak *et al.,* 2004). It leads to a negative relationship between profitability and external equities. Nevertheless, despite a broad discussion on the positive and negative association of debt and profitability, Krishnan and Moyer (1996), Fattouh *et al* (2005) and Nguyen and Ramachandran (2006) could not confirm that profitability is a significant factor in the leverage decision.

Ross *et al.,* (1999) argue that enterprises profitability can be measured in two ways. These are accounting-based measures and economic-based measures. The main difference between these two measures of enterprises profitability is; economic-based profitability always accounts for risk and it implies that a firm is profitable only if its profitability is greater than investors can achieve independently in the capital market. While accounting-based measures exclude the involvement of risk, concepts and risk related matters (Skrepnek, 2004).

Ross *et al.* (1999) also proposed some methods and techniques to measure profitability including profit margin or return on sales, return on assets, and return on equity. Previous research has used several different ratios to measure SMEs profitability depending on respective research goals. For example, Hutchinson *et al,* (1988) measures SME profitability using earnings before interest and tax/total assets ratio, net profit after tax/owners' equity and net profit after tax/sales ratio. Burns (1985) uses three ratios; return on net assets, return on total assets and return on equity. Table 3.1 illustrates the techniques and approaches used by previous researchers to measure profitability of SMEs.

Table 3.1: Summary of measurement of SME profitability

Scholar(s) and year	Proportion	Estimation/Measurement
Jaggi & Considine (1990)	Return on assets	Operating profit/Total assets
Laitinen (1992)	Return on investment	Return on investment ratio

Meric *et al.* (1997)	Return on assets	Net income/Total assets
	Return on equity	Net income/Common equity
	Return on sales	Operating profit/Sales
Meric and Meric (1992)	Return on sales	Net profit after tax/Sales
	Return on assets	Earnings before interest and tax/Total assets
	Return on equity	Net profit after tax/Owners' equity
Burns (1985)	Return on total assets	Measure of firm's efficient use of assets
	Return on equity	A measure of the profit return to the shareholders
	Return on net asset	The key measure of performance

Source: Compiled from the following literatures (Jaggi & Considine, 1990; Laitinen, 1992; Meric *et al.*, 1997; Meric and Meric, 1988; Burns, 1985)

In general, there are a number of factors influencing enterprise profitability. From the economic profit, measuring viewpoint Table 3.2 summarises key factors that influence SME profitability based on different researchers' viewpoints.

Table 3.2: Summary of literature review of main factors affecting SME profitability

Scholar(s) and year	Main factors affecting profitability
McDonald (1999)	Firms Union density, import penetration, real wage inflation, Firm market share
Laitinen (1992)	Return on investment ratio
Westerfield and Jaffe (1999), Cohen (1989)	Revenue, costs and capital.
Lev (1983)	type of product, degree of competition, degree of capital intensity as well as firm size
Burns (1985)	Many economic factors like

Kirchhoff and Kirchhoff (1987)	Family contributions, wage and salary expense and Revenue

Source: Compiled from the following literatures (McDonald, 1999; Laitinen, 1992; Westerfield and Jaffe, 1999; Lev, 1983; Burns, 1985, 1988; Burns, 1985; Kirchhoff and Kirchhoff, 1987)

3.5.3 BANK CREDIT AND ENTERPRISE PERFORMANCE

Extensive researches (Nichter and Goldmark, 2009; Butler & Cornaggia, 2007; Lashitew, 2011; Badia & Slootmaekers, 2008; Olutunla & Obamuyi, 2008; Gebrehiwot & Wolday, 2006; Love, 2003; Wurgler, 2000; Nguyen and Ramachandran, 2006; Newman *et al.,* 2011; Borgia and Newman, 2012; Emecheta & Ibe, 2014) have attempted to assess the determining factors of SME performance. Most of them agree that financial access is a key determining factor to enhance enterprise performance in terms of boosting productivity and profitability. For example, Nichter and Goldmark (2009) found that access to bank credit is the main determining factor for the growth of micro and small enterprises.

This result is similar to those of several studies that find significant contribution of finance access on SMEs performance (Gebrehiwot & Wolday, 2006; Love, 2003; Wurgler, 2000). Some authors attribute large productivity improvements to access to credit (Butler & Cornaggia, 2007; Lashitew, 2011; Badia & Slootmaekers, 2008), while others report that credit access does not have any bottom line impact on firm profitability and productivity (Hanson, 2001). Most studies focus either on cross-country analyses or in a specific sector.

Recent theoretical research (Lashitew, 2011) demonstrates that credit access used as firm-level financial access has significant negative effect on the cost of capital. This research result shows that access to credit allows firms to employ more capital in order to boost SME productivity and profit. Moreover, the above study suggests that reduction in the firm's operation costs could come directly from investing in more productive capital equipment whereby increased demand could stimulate and improve the expansion of enterprise performance. Moreover, researchers' findings indicate that access to external finance may allow firms to have better capacity to acquire necessary working capital and technical inputs, and that could allow firms to have favourable impacts on SMEs productivity and growth (Petersen and Rajan, 2002; Nguyen and Ramachandran, 2006).

Butler and Cornaggia (2007) share a similar view in an experimentally based study that examines the relation between access to finance and productivity at the country level. They adopt the triple difference (DIDID) testing approach and find that productivity increases in countries with relatively strong access to finance. It implies a positive relationship between access to finance and enterprise productivity. More specifically their study illustrates that access to finance, particularly bank credit, has a strong positive effect on firms' productivity and profitability. This result is statistically significant and robust to a variety of controls, alternative variables, and tests and it confirms that firms that are credit constrained exhibit poorer performance and productivity.

Other research by Badia and Slootmaekers (2008) develops a methodology that corrects misspecification problems of previous studies. It shows that young and highly indebted firms tend to be more financially constrained. More importantly, for most sectors, financial constraints do lower firm productivity, where the dampening effect of financial constraints on productivity is remarkably large.

Other empirical research (Gatti & Love, 2006; Butler and Cornaggia; 2007) discovered the causal effects of access to finance upon firm productivity using data from a cross section of Bulgarian firms. The statistical significance of the level of SME productivity and the degree of confidence is the true relationship that is close to the estimated relationship. Hence, the study concluded that credit is positively and strongly associated with the total factor productivity (TFP). Most macroeconomic literatures highlight the importance of financial market to the productivity growth of SMEs (Sleuwaegen & Goedhuys, 2002; Babajid, 2012; Alfaro *et al.*, 2009). In addition, Demirguk (2006), Beck *&* Laoayz (1999), and Ang and McKibbini (2006) also assert that finance is the key determining factor for SMEs productivity and growth.

Other studies report that credit access does not have any bottom line impact on productivity Reyes *et al.*, 2012; Ghani & Suri, 1999; Hanson, 2001; Malesky & HH, 2009; Allen *et al.*, 2012). Researchers like Soderbom (2012), Bigsten and Gebreeyesus (2009), and Bigsten and Gebreeyesus (2007), have analysed issues related to the productivity of the manufacturing sector in Ethiopia. Other research shows that the direction of causality between access to finance and SME productivity performance runs both ways, especially for developing economies (Ghani & Suri, 1999). Hanson (2001) argues that there is weak evidence that access to finance generates positive impacts on firm productivity.

Similarly, a study conducted by Reyes *et al.* (2012), focused on panel data from a survey of 177 farmers in Chile, found that short-term credit does not have an impact on farms productivity. This research only focused on the effect of short-term credit on firm's productivity for market-oriented farmers. As a result, the question at what extent and level access to credit have a real effect on SME profitability especially in developing country's context is inconclusive and still there is a gap for the research effort (EEA, 2015).

In general, the previous empirical study (Gatti & Love, 2006) supported the hypothesis that access to finance makes a significant positive impact on productivity at country, sector and firm levels. However, the exact channels through which finance affects the growth are not yet well understood and results are mixed. Some of the research findings (Rahaman, 2011; Cecchetti & Kharroubi, 2012; Beck & Demirguc-Kunt, 2006; Shariff *et al.*, 2010; Shariff & Peou, 2008; Newman, 2010) underlined that a well-developed credit access to business firms can influence the level of savings, firm's investment decisions, and productivity that could be a catalyst for technological innovation.

The level and degree to which measurable productivity outcomes are influenced by the variables of quality, quantity, sustainability and suitability to the specific market constraints remain challenging areas for (Badia & Slootmaekers, 2008) research. There are not sufficient studies that have examined this issue from a provider's perspective or even from a developing economy setting (Beck and Laoayz, 1999).

Similarly, much research results in developed countries context reveals that SME productivity growth and credit access has direct relationship (Nichter & Goldmark, 2009; Gebrehiwot & Wolday, 2006; Lora & Pages, 2011; Love, 2003; Wurgler, 2000). This effect is not clear while considering developing countries context since, there is no study has empirically explored well the effect of finance on the productivity and profitability performance of SMEs in Sub-Saharan Africa country's context particularly in Ethiopia (Asiedu *et al.,* 2013).

3.6 CONCLUSION

Generally, prior researchers provide detailed insights into the determining factors for improving SME productivity. The comprehensive exploration showed that credit access could contribute positively to SME productivity and profitability, which is influenced by various factors at the macro and micro economic levels. However, the majority of the literature is based on theoretical assertions with fewer sources having empirical basis in developed countries contexts. This highlights a gap that needs to be filled by undertaking empirical studies in developing countries contexts like Ethiopia.

CHAPTER 4: STUDY METHODOLOGY AND FRAMWORKE

4.1 INTRODUCTION

The previous chapter (i.e. chapter three), introduced finance development and firms' performance align with the theories that extensively discuss the impacts of finance on the firms' performance and growth. Assessment of the literature reveals that the pecking order model together with life cycle, trade-off, and productivity theories can contribute to developing a better understanding of the impacts of access to external finance on the SMEs' performance.

This chapter summarises all the constructs reviewed into a broad conceptual framework and develops hypotheses to be tested in the data analysis. Moreover, it presents the methodology used in the empirical component of the current study. It describes and justifies the methods techniques and steps used to address the principal research question stated by the study. The methodology covers issues that relate to the type of data utilised, the way it was collected and analysed.

4.2 CONCEPTUAL FRAMWORK

The conceptual framework for this study is developed based upon the gaps identified in the literature review, specifically those related to access to external finance and SMEs performances. The potential relationship between access to credit and SMEs productivity and profitability performance is explained below by a flowchart (Figure 4.1) and it illustrates the determining factors of SME productivity and profitability. The mutually benefitting relationship between SMEs in the manufacturing sector and enabling environment for their production processes is described on the framework. Dalberg (2011) stated that the linkages between enterprise performance and business enabling environments are described as strong if productivity is enhanced through strong economic linkages, in the form of improving access to finance.

The conceptual framework of the study follows and considers the view of Osei-Assibey (2013), who asserts that access to bank credit influences firm performance indirectly through different channels. The author further argued that access to bank credit improves firm productivity and profitability by acting as an enabler for the drivers of productivity. In support of the above idea Wolf (2007) also argue that access to credit enables firms to take business advantage and invest in new technology, undertake new business opportunities, train workers and to invest in high quality inputs all of which are necessary in improving firm's productivity and profitability performance.

According to picking order theory, there are different types of finance sources (i.e. formal; informal; external; internal). The focus of this study however, is mainly relay on formal sources of finance (i.e. bank credit, box 2), cost of finance to SMEs (i.e. interest rate, box 9) will also likely be higher due to a number of factors previously listed that limit access to funding and SME productivity and profitability performance (i.e. SME performance, box 8).

Access to credit and firm productivity and profitability performance

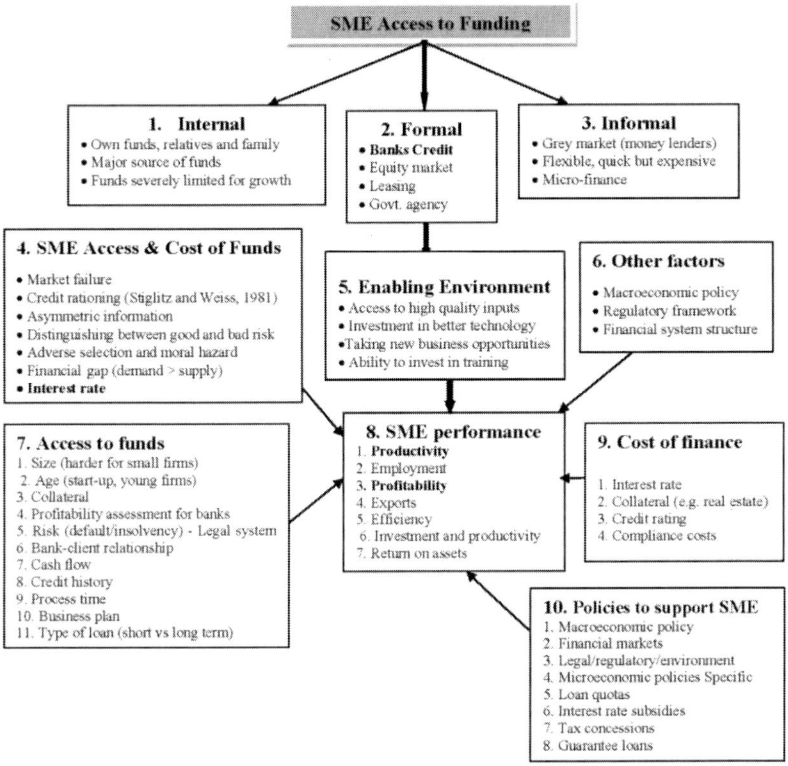

Figure 4.1: Conceptual Framework

Source: Author's conceptualization based on Osei-Assibey (2013) and Wolf (2007).

From the above conceptual frame work figure the study mainly rely on the following variables bank credit from (box two); interest rate from (box four); productivity and profitability from (box eight).

The conceptual framework for this research, depicted in Figure 4.1, represents the model of the effects of access to bank credit on SME productivity and profitability performance. It indicates that SME productivity is expected to be positively influenced by efficient access to bank credit. The conceptual framework illustrates the systematic ways to test for the hypothesis.

4.3 METHODOLOGY

The first section of the research methodology starts by discussing the research paradigm, research design and research approach. It then moves to describe and justify the specific research methods and procedures used in analysing the link between credit access and SMEs performance. It also describes the data sources, how it was collected and a justification of the statistical tests used in the analysis.

4.3.1 RESEARCH PARADIGM AND DESGIN

According to du Plooy (2009:19), a research paradigm is a set of ideas or theory that guides the research by establishing a set of practices. In general, different disciplines tend to be governed by particular paradigms, for example, paradigms like positivism (Saarani and Shahadan, 2013). Morgan (2007:50-54) identified four different *paradigms, which are paradigms as worldviews, as epistemological stances, as shared beliefs among members of a specialty area and as model examples of research.* All versions treat paradigms as shared belief systems that influence the kind of knowledge researchers seek and how they interpret it. This study is multidisciplinary, hence pragmatic, as it combines aspects from many disciplines, which demands a combination of diverse research methods.

This research is designed under a broadly positivist paradigm. Collis and Hussey (2003) state that a positivist researcher is likely to be concerned with ensuring that any concept's use can be operationalised; that is, described in such a way that they can be measured. This study designed to follow this paradigm since; a positivist study helps to rely heavily on quantitative and manipulative methods. It takes a deductive approach and that is in line with most previous studies on the area of finance and firms productivity and profitability performance (for example, Ghosh, 2006; Levine, 2001; Robin &

Pande, 2005; Beck, *et al.*, 2005), this study adopts a positivist paradigm for the following reasons:

- The ontological assumptions of objectivism better match the researcher's assumptions about the nature of reality. The researcher assumes the existence of a world of cause and effect. To make more clear, the assumption is that there are some realities "i.e. the performance of any firms determined by a number of factors", which exist in the world and it may affect enterprises productivity and profitability performance. Therefore, the study follow a realistic ontology and the view it as a fundamental reality. Pring (2004:62) referred to this notion saying, "one purpose of research is to explain what is the case or what has happened" that is a reason for seeking explanations.
- In one or another, this study also follows the theoretical perspective and adopted different relevant theories and models that is developed by a number of researchers (e.g. productivity theory, profit maximization theory, pecking order theory, trade-off theory, agency theory, and life-cycle model). Theoretical perspective of deductive study that allows the researcher to develop hypotheses and test those using empirical data and it is appropriate, as recommended by Saunders *et al* (2009). If the empirical data is drawn from a sufficiently large random sample, the statistical results of a positivist study can be generalised from the sample to the population under study. The results are likely to be high in reliability, which means that if another researcher replicates the study the same results are likely to be achieved (Collis and Hussey, 2003).

Figure 4.2 shows the various steps undertaken in designing the study. Based on the research objectives and research questions, the steps include deciding which information to collect (variables), where was it to be collected (study area), from who (the target population), how was it collected (methods), and how was it analysed (data analysis).

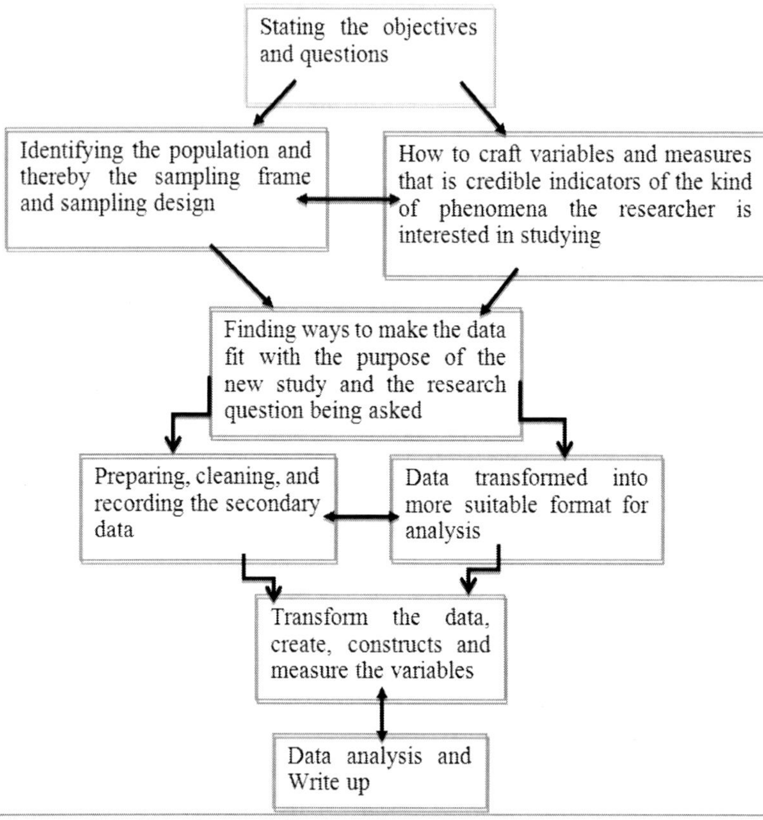

Figure 4.2: Design of the study
Source: Adapted from Patel *et al.* (2004:159)

4.3.2 RESEARCH APPROACH

The research can be classified as descriptive, analytic, exploratory and predictive research (Baxter & Babbie, 2004). The most appropriate research approach for this study is exploratory and descriptive. This research examines and quantifies how access to finance affects the level of SME performance in a developing country context, which is a relatively inconclusive field of enquiry (see Chapter 3). Research design follows research approach, from which there are four types to select survey, experiment, observation and secondary data (Murthy & Bhojanna, 2008).

Choosing a type of research approach is based on the advantages and disadvantages of each approach and circumstances in which the research problem is defined. In this research, the survey data and quantitative-method approach is used to examine the effects of access to bank credit on the SME performance that is measured in terms of productivity and profitability level. The necessary variables to estimate the level of SMEs profitability and productivity performance are derived from the data.

In terms of research technique, this research uses survey data that were gathered by the Central Statistical Agency (CSA) of Ethiopia prior to the current needs of this study (to view the survey questionnaire (see Appendix F). The advantage of using this data and the argument for choosing survey data is based on the followings four major reasons.

- Firstly, the survey data is much coincides with the purpose of this study and the data align with the topic areas.
- Secondly, this survey data has comprehensive source of information that this study want to collect and it has a kind of data that align with the focus of this study.
- Thirdly, the survey data is collected at country level and it has large coverage area.
- Fourth, since, Central Statistics Agency (CSA) of Ethiopia collected the survey. Hence the source is reliable and of high credentials. In general, this survey data provides a quick, efficient and accurate means of assessing information about the population of this study. It is more appropriate and fortunately, it is available and accessible.

4.4 DESCRIPTIONS OF VARIABLES

In developing a variable association model and testing the hypothesis of relationship, there are two kinds of variables involved: dependent/response and independent/explanatory variables (Lewis-Beck, 1974). The dependent/response variable is the presumed effect, whereas independent/ explanatory variables are the presumed causes (ibid). Dependent variables are variables that are to be expected or explained and independent variables are variables believed to affect the dependent variable (Zikmund, 1997). This is the variable, the researcher, will manipulate to see if it makes the dependent variable change.

SMEs productivity and profitability are abstract concepts that are analysed as the dependent variables and cannot be measured directly. The study has adopted 'Cobb-Dauglas production function' with three input variables (capital, labour and material inputs) in order to estimate the level of SMEs productivity with and without access to bank credit. Therefore, these factor inputs are independent variables for the study. In addition, the efficiency of access to finance (bank credit) is viewed as an independent variable. However, credit is not an endogenous variable in the production process then, it is not determined by the model and it requires multi-dimensional construct.

In the production function, model output is the dependent variable and is measured as total value of product (total sales minus expenditure on materials) and the three independent variables are labour, capital and material input. Labour is measured by the number of employees in an enterprise and amount of total wage while capital is measured as the total book value of the fixed assets, whereas material inputs are measured by the value of total raw materials.

On the other hand, in the linear, dynamic mathematical model, profitability is the dependent variable and is measured as total sales minus expenditure on materials. The key independent or explanatory variable in the profitability estimation model are bank loan; level of sales; age of business; firm size and interest rates. Respectively bank loan is measured by the amount of loan obtained by the firm on time. Sale variable is measured by the total level of sales by the specific firm at time *t*. Age of the business is measured by the number of years by specific firm at time *t*. Enterprises age is captured by number of years an enterprise has existed. Enterprises age may be important in explaining variation in productivity among firms (Gatti and Love, 2006). The number of employee at time t measures size of firm's and interest rate is measured by amount of credit cost at the time *t*. These two categories of variables known to influence the firm's performance in terms of productivity and profitability performance (Gatti and Love, 2006, Mario, 2015).

The other sets of variables are; variables with formal finance access attributes and enterprise specific attributes. Enterprise specific attributes used in this study like age of the enterprise, business activity or type of industry and ownership structure. Ownership is measured by three dummy variables showing enterprises ownership like privately owned firm, public owned firm private firms and government owned firm. The dummy for private owned firm is equal to 1 if enterprise owned by government is equal to 2 and 0 if otherwise.

The effect of the types of sectors activity type on productivity is unknown and will be determined in the model. According to Moyi (2013), different production activity could be subject to specific activity-related circumstances that could lead to differences in performance. In this study, there are no sector specific dummy variables because the target group of the study belongs to one sector, which is manufacturing enterprises.

Terms used in this study include SMEs, credit, firm productivity, and firm profitability. SMEs have the same definition given by the World Bank and uses number of employees as criteria (see Section 2.6).

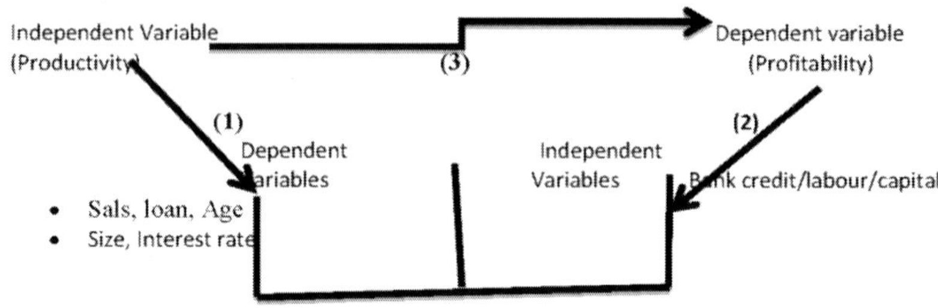

Figure 4.3 Variables and their respective classification.
Source: Adapted from Lewis-Beck (1974)

Figure 4.3 summarizes all variables used in the study and it shows their possible interactions. There are key points or observations to be noted in the figure. It shows that the study has two distinct models to measure SMEs productivity and profitability separately. Each estimation model has its own dependent and independent variables. The arrow shows that dependent variables are those variables provide a response for the influence through production or business process.

The first dependent variable of interest in this study is SME productivity. The productivity of SME considered from period 2005 to 2012. The second dependent variable of interest is SME profitability. Under SME productivity analysis, this study considers labour, capital and material inputs as the main independent variables and other controlling instrumental variables like age and size of the business, ownership type and credit. SMEs age is measured as the log of years of firm in the market; firm size is defined and measured by the number of employees, instrumented variables are bank credit firms with guarantees and utility expenses respectively (Cameron and Trivedi, 2005).

Whereas, in the profitability estimation model amount of sales, loan, interest rate, size and age of SME are taken as independent variables. Bank credit is a dichotomous (yes, no) variable where yes means the enterprise has a credit or revolving credit facility from a commercial bank. In a business context, credit is a financial transaction/communication and is the purchase of the present value of money with the promise to pay the obligations in the future according to a pre-arranged agreement and at a specified cost defined by the interest rate. World Bank (2001) defined credit as the power or ability to obtain goods or services in exchange for a promise to pay later. Similarly, it is a power or ability to obtain money by the borrowing process, in return for a promise to repay the obligations in the future.

Other important independent variable in estimation of SMEs productivity model is interest rate. The role of interest rate in traditional monetary theory had viewed as any other input price (Baltensperge and Devinne, 1985). While not really getting for analysing this issue, the availability doctrine at least addressed the profitability that the interest rate was different from the price of a homogeneous good. Discussing the non-price term of loan contracts (credit standards) as non-temporary events it was implicitly treating such factors as equilibrium phenomena and not simply as artefacts of an adjustment process

Below is the detailed description of the dependent and independent variables that are defined and utilised in this study. The key explanatory and response variables used for this study are summarized below in tabular form.

Table 4.1: Variables used in the ordered fixed regression model

Independent variables	Variable name in the model	Expected relationship
Output (total value of production)	Y	- /+
Labour (amount of wage total)	L	+

Capita (total book value of the fixed assets at the beginning of the year)	K	+
Material inputs (Value of total raw materials)	M	+

Source: Constructed based on the hypothesis stated above for the current study.

Table 4.2: Variables used in the ordered fixed regression model

Independent variables	Variable name in the model	Expected relationship
Profit response variable for firm j at time t	π	+
Level of sales by firm j at time t	Sale	+
Age of business by firm j at time t	age	-/+
Size of firm by the number of employees at time t (Total permanent employees") is used to measure the size of business)	size	-/+
Interest(interest rate at time t)	Interest	-

Source: Constructed based on the hypothesis and from the current study assumption

4.5 HYPOTHESES STATEMENTS

In theory the inherent existence of the profit in the business market is serious owners should induce competitiveness and improve their performance which translates into improved total factors of productivity and profitability (Syverson, 2011). Previous studies have evidenced the importance of credit access in influencing the performance of firms. Empirically, the overall direction supports positive and negative associations of credit access and firms performance with long-term leverage and short-term leverage, respectively (see Romano *et al.,* 2000; Hall *et al.,* 2004; Zou and Xiao, 2006; Vos *et al.,* 2007; Frank and Goyal, 2009; Bany-Ariffin *et al.,* 2010; Booth *et al.,* 2001; Bevan and Danbolt, 2002; Cassar and Holmes, 2003; Chen, 2004; Sogorb-Mira, 2005; Fattouh *et al.,* 2005; Ortqvist *et al.,* 2006; Klapper *et al.,* 2006). On the other hand, some studies have found a negative association between credit access and firms productivity and profitability performance (Nguyen and Ramachandran, 2006; Sayilgan *et al.,* 2006; Qian *et al.,* 2009; Li *et al.,* 2009; Karadeniz *et al.,* 2009.

Modigliani and Miller (1958) expected no association between the access to credit and firms performance. However, Modigliani and Miller (1963) and trade-off theory predicted positive association between access to credit and firms performance. In contrast, agency theory expects a negative association between credit level and firm's performance. Despite inconclusive evidence on the issue, this study assumes that access to bank credit may lead to good performance of the firm. Accordingly, this study proposes the following general hypothesis:

> Small and Medium sized Enterprises that are run by individuals who have access to bank credit must have a higher level of total factor productivity and profitability than enterprises operating without bank credit.

Hypothesis testing involves the careful construction of two statements: the null hypothesis and the alternative hypothesis (Andrea, 2009). The null hypothesis is what the research attempts to overturn by the hypothesis test whereas alternative hypothesis is what is demonstrated in an indirect way by the use of the hypothesis test (Lewis-Beck, 1974; Dixon and Massey, 1983). If the null hypothesis is rejected, then the alternative hypothesis will be accepted (Boland, 2000; Hamilton, 2013). In other words, if the null hypothesis is not rejected, then the alternative hypothesis is not accepted. The general study hypothesis stated above can be decomposed into two parts, namely null and alternative. Hence, the null hypothesis and alternative hypothesis adopted for this study are as follows:

H_0: **Finance access has no contribution to improve SMEs productivity** and profitability

H_1: Finance access improves productivity and profitability of SMEs in Ethiopia.

4.6 DATA COLLECTION AND METHODS

This section discusses data sources and the measurement of key variables. Although, the study supplementary data derived from other sources (National Bank of Ethiopia), much of the data for analysis comes from the Central Statistics Agency (CSA) of Ethiopian Manufacturing Survey dataset. The study will, therefore, describe the CSA dataset and introduce the variables used for measuring the effects of bank credit access on SMEs productivity and profitability performance.

4.6.1 DATA

This study makes use of the 2005-2012 nationwide raw survey data on manufacturing industries collected by the Central Statistical Agency (CSA) of Ethiopia. This database contains financial and economic information on manufacturing enterprises in Ethiopia. CSA of Ethiopia has been publishing manufacturing industry survey data results on annual basis since 1968 E.C. to provide users with reliable, comprehensive and timely statistical data on these sectors (CSA, 2011). This survey, which is conducted on annual basis, is the principal source of industrial statistics in the country. The scope of this manufacturing survey is confined to those establishments which engage ten persons and above and use power-driven machinery and covers both public and private industries in all regions of the country, where establishments under the scope of the survey are found.

The raw manufacturing survey dataset includes information on quantity and unit prices of the firms' products, capital, labour, raw material, energy inputs as well as investment and other industrial costs. It also incorporates detailed information on sales, employment, use of raw materials, energy, investment, depreciation and stock of capital, access to credit, access to output market (local and export), type of ownership, number of years in business and the conditions of accounting record keeping. Moreover, there are information on enterprise revenue as a rough proxy for expected income, capital at the beginning of the year for collateral, age of the enterprise for possible lending relationship and conditions of accounting record keeping for availability of enterprise credit information.

The survey data has detailed information on firm performance and productivity (material inputs, sales, labour and capital) as well as firms' ratings on various aspects of the business environment. Although this study relies on manufacturing data only, the survey targets both manufacturing and electricity industries that are formally registered and have ten or more employees. It has detailed information on number of establishments, number of persons engaged, and employees, wages and salaries paid by major industrial groups, sex, nationality and occupation, paid-up capital, gross value of production, industrial and non-industrial costs, value added, operating surplus, quantity of production and raw materials consumed, fixed assets, investment and production capacity are presented.

For this study, the major advantage of using the CSA of Ethiopia manufacturing raw survey data is that it has list of the types of data that align with the focus of this study and the study need to collect. Moreover, the data is conducted systematically using standardized survey questionnaires and instruments (see Appendix F). It can be useful to this study because the data is comprehensive source of information that usually covers long periods. The dataset thus provides comparable information that is unique for its extensive regional coverage.

A number of quality control steps were taken by this study to ensure the quality of data. The first step taken in this direction was, to revise and check the questionnaire, to make it easier for internal consistency checking or editing, both at analysis and at estimation level. In addition, before collecting the raw data from CSA the study has determined which institutions conduct research on the topic area or country in question. After, knowing the purpose of data collection it helped to evaluate the quality of the data and discern the potential level of bias

In addition, a preliminary list of data sources was analyzed and a list of the types of data that the study needs to collect was obtained from relevant data source. Having a well-defined purpose, a clear understanding of why the study is collecting the data and of what kind of data the study wants to collect, analyze, and better understand could helped the study to remain focused and prevent the study from becoming overwhelmed with the volume of the data.

4.6.2 TARGET POPULATION

According to Zikmund, (1997) definition, the target population is the complete group of individuals under study units or cases that are relevant to the research. In this study, the scope of the manufacturing survey data confined to those establishments that engage ten and more persons and use power-driven machinery. It covers both public and private industries in all regions of the country, where establishments under the scope of the survey are found. Therefore, the target population in this research is all manufacturing enterprises data covered by the Central Statistics Agency (CSA) between the years 2005 to 2012.

4.6.3 SAMPLING METHOD

The study uses purposive or judgmental sampling method and considered World Bank Small and Medium enterprises definition criteria to choose sample SMEs. The sample data were selected from the total population of 2,682 manufacturing enterprises that engage more than 10 and less than 99 persons.

4.6.4 SAMPLE SIZE

The data contains a number of manufacturing industries and its respective information. Manufacturing enterprises that have been covered by the survey includes Food & Beverages, Textiles and Footwear, Cement, Printing & Publishing, Iron, Plastics & Rubber, Chemicals and Pharmaceuticals. It is mentioned already that, the total enterprises within this population are 2,682. The data also incorporates detailed information on enterprises sales, access to credit, access to output markets (local and export), employment, entrepreneurial capability, use of raw materials and energy, investment, depreciation and stock of capital, type of ownership, number of years in business and the conditions of accounting record keeping. By applying purposive sampling technique only enterprises with an employment level of 10 to 99 persons were considered and a sample of 1,542 manufacturing enterprises are drawn for further analysis.

4.6.5 DATA TRANSFORMATION

Data collected for manufacturing SMEs between the years 2005 to 2012 is transformed into a more suitable spreadsheet format like Microsoft Excel software. After data processing, the Statistics Package for Social Science (SPSS) and STAT are utilised for data analysis. Statistical techniques used in this study include descriptive and inference statistics.

4.6.6 DATA ANALYSIS

The rationale of analytic methods is to transform data into information needed to make decisions. The choice of the methods of statistical analysis depends on the objectives of the study and the questions to answer (Onwuegbuzie and Collins, 2007). The variables also used to determine whether the statistical techniques applied should be univariates data analysis, bi-variant data analysis or multivariate data analysis.

This study is concerned with three main research questions. The *first* is how important is access to finance to improve Small and Medium Manufacturing Enterprise productivity and profitability in Ethiopia? The *second* is how does access to bank credit affect productivity and profitability of Small and Medium Manufacturing Enterprises in developing countries like Ethiopia? The *third* is to what extent, access to finance influences SME productivity and profitability performance in developing countries context hence, descriptive statistics and hypothesis testing are the two main methods of data analysis that are suitable to these research questions. Specifically, multiple linear regressions are developed and tested to explain the relationships between bank credit and SME productivity and profitability.

The study conducted by Stieglitz (1947) demonstrated that if the market were under a perfect competitive condition, firm's value would not be affected by their financial decisions. However, the perfect market condition does not practically hold illustrated that under the imperfect market condition, credit access affect the firm's productivity and profitability. Moreover, transaction cost theory demonstrates that business enterprises and trading partners use credit to economize costs of exchanges. A business owner tries to minimize their transaction costs that are associated with uncertain business environments (World Bank 2001c).

Several theories explain the determinants of access to credit (Ng *et al.,* 2007), and they establish a theoretical model to evaluate the effects of bank credit. For example, the transaction theory points out that bank credit can reduce exchange costs by separating goods exchanges from money exchanges (ibid). Nevertheless, those credit theories lack empirical evidences to support them. Little research specifically focuses on the understanding of the relationship between bank credit and firm's profitability and productivity performance. In this study, the researcher tries to bridge this gap.

4.6.7 DESCRIPTIVE STATISTICS

Descriptive statistics are used to describe the characteristics of the sample, to check the variables for making assumption violation and to address specific research questions (Pallant, 2011). The aim of undertaking descriptive statistics is to establish patterns, relationships and to describe variables. The patterns and structures in the data are discovered through the distribution of single variables and by relationships between variables (Adèr & Mellenbergh, 1999). In this study, the preliminary analysis and descriptive statistics are performed using SPSS 17.0. The descriptive statistics comprise univariate analysis in which data for single variables are analysed individually (Cramer, 1994:15). These include frequencies, proportions, means, percentages, graphs, and charts. These statistics were used to describe all the important variables in the study. The results are presented in the following chapters.

4.7 ANALYTICAL MODEL

For the purpose of this study SMEs are divided into two groups. In the first group there are SMEs that have access to bank credit and in the second there are group of SMEs that use informal sources of finance for normal operation. The study follows the methodology developed by (Ferri, 1981) under the assumption that banks can offer better credit terms. It is examined whether firms with access to bank credit have relatively higher levels of total factor productivity and profitability performance than the group of firms operating without access to bank credit.

The main components of the analytical model for this study are constructed to estimate SMEs productivity and profitability. This study follows neoclassical production assumption for specifying the relationship between inputs, efficiency and outputs by applying Cobb-Douglass production function. In addition, a linear, dynamic mathematical model is used to estimate SMEs profitability.

According to (Baily *et al.,* 1992) firms' total factor productivity can be examined through estimating major production inputs (i.e. capital, labour, material inputs, energy inputs) and estimating returns to these inputs with and without access to bank credit. On the other hand, enterprises profitability can be measured through estimating returns on investment (Stierwald, 2010)

Many scholars (Le and Nguyen, 2009; Newman, 2010; Borgia and Newman, 2012; Osei-Assibey, 2013) argue that access to credit influences enterprises productivity and profitability indirectly through different channels. For example Osei-Assibey (2013), asserts that access to credit improve enterprises productivity and profitability performance by acting as an enabler for the drivers of productivity. According to Wolf (2007), access to credit also allows enterprises to take advantage of new business opportunities, to train and empower workers. Moreover, it helps to invest in new technology and to acquire high quality production processing inputs, all of which are necessary in improving firm's productivity. The relationship between access to credit and SME productivity and profitability are illustrated below by a flowchart (Figure 4.4).

This analytical model for the current study can be expressed in mathematical notation illustrated in section 4.7.2 below. First, SMEs are divided into two groups that have access to bank credit and a group of firms that use informal sources of finance for normal operation. Under the assumption that banks can offer better credit terms, it is examined whether firms with access to bank credit have relatively higher levels of TFP than the group of firms without access to bank credit.

Figure 4.4: Analytical model for the research study

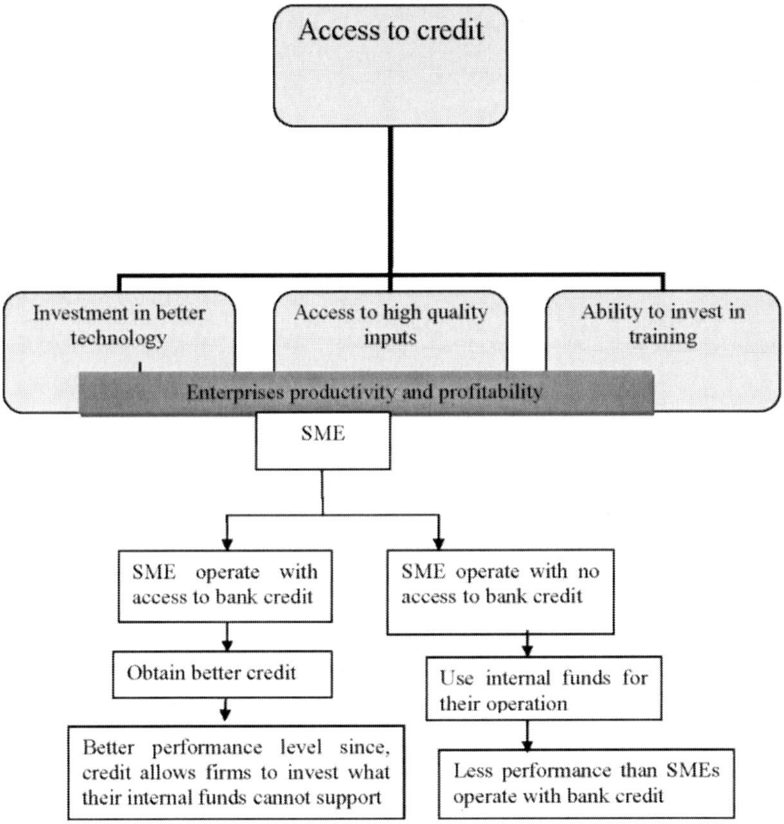

Source: Own conceptualization based on Osei-Assibey (2013) and Wolf (2007).

4.7.1 MODEL SPECIFICATION

This section tests empirically the hypothesis that bank credit improves enterprises' productivity and profitability. To do this initially, enterprises that engage more than ten and less than hundred persons are identified from the manufacturing survey dataset. With these, two groups of enterprises are formed. One group includes only enterprises with access to bank credit and the other group enterprises use alternative sources of finance for its production process. Under the assumption that banks can offer better credit terms, it is examined whether enterprises with access to bank credit have relatively higher levels of productivity than the other group of firms (Berger and Udell, 1995; Rajan and Zingales, 1995).

Moreover, this study uses two distinct multiple regression models and techniques in order to analyse the effect of bank credit on SME productivity and profitability unconnectedly and designed two respective econometric models to developed the hypothesis of association between different variables mainly access to bank credit and SME productivity and profitability.

The first model follows Cobb-Douglas production function to estimate SMEs productivity. The second model constructed based on linear, dynamic mathematical model with the objective of estimating SMEs profitability performance in response with access to bank credit. These distinct models revealed that different independent variables had varied relationships with the level of credit access. In other words, factors that were significantly influence the level of SMEs productivity and profitability were different for each group.

Accordingly, SMEs productivity can be analysed through estimations of enterprises Total Factor Productivity (TFP) and it can only be captured as the residual between the actual output and inputs estimated by an appropriate production function. Consequently, the estimation of TFP may be susceptible to measurement errors. A direct estimation of the production function can provide a good robustness check for the indirect estimation of a TFP estimation model.

SMEs profitability can be analysed and estimated in accordance with related literature and the study follow the methodology developed by (Olutunla & Obamuyi, 2008) and used a linear, dynamic mathematical model. The equation specifies profitability as the dependent variable, and loans, sales, age of business, size of business and interest rate as independent variables. The equation measures the level of SMEs profitability on the bases of returns on investment and other key measures of performance.

In this study, three different models that have been estimated using the above-mentioned variables can measure SMEs Total Factor Productivity (TFP):

1 Basic model where the input-output variables are directly applied to the production function.
2 A second model where material inputs and capital are lumped together in the model to consider the fact that loans/credit can be used to finance raw material purchases.
3 A third model where a host of control variables are introduced such as the age of enterprise, ownership type, industry type and region to control the effect of enterprise-specific factors.

4.2 ECONOMETRIC ANALYSIS

4.2.1 ESTIMATION OF SME PRODUCTIVITY

There are many ways for measuring SMEs Total Factor Productivity (TFP). However, the estimation of it takes into account of multi-factors but entails various methodological concerns depending on the assumptions the researcher willing to make. In general, a Cobb-Douglass production function is most often used in empirical research to estimate firm's productivity since; it is based on the statistical observation (Fadejeva and Melihous, 2009). Moreover, the method adopted to estimate SMEs TFP in this study is similar to the approach used by Gatti and Love (2008). The total factors of production level for SMEs is obtained as the difference between actual output levels and output predicted from estimates of a Cobb-Douglas production function. In calculating SME's TFP, this study specifies a general production function that captures the relationship between inputs and outputs.

To estimate SMEs total factor productivity with respect to access to credit this study is following Solow's growth theory (Solow, 1957) and applying Cobb-Douglas production function. In productivity theory, if the factor like markets is competitive, then the marginal product of each input equals its factor prices and that is called 'coefficients of respective factor inputs' (Felipe and Adams, 2005). This assumption and the adopted model will help to estimate and compare the level of SMEs TFP and returns to capital, returns to labour and raw material inputs across the two groups of (with and without access to bank credit) enterprises during a given survey year. In level form efficiency this is represented as the expected value of TFP, the estimated residual is obtained by calculating the difference between actual and predicted firms output. Moreover, TFP is estimated by approximating the weighted sum of the inputs from the estimation of Cobb-Douglas production function based on the Solow growth theory (Solow, 1957) and it is stated in the following form:

$$Y_i = E_i K_i^{\alpha k} L_i^{\alpha l} M_i^{\alpha m} \ldots\ldots\ldots\ldots\ldots\ldots (1)$$

Equation (1) is a Cobb-Douglass production function (by assumption) (Felipe and Adams. (2005). Where Y_i is firms output of the ith firm; K_i , L_i and M_i represent capital, labour and material inputs respectively and E_i captures firm level efficiency.

Transform the above general cobb-Dauglas production function in to a linear form by taking natural logarithms on both sides of the equation. The general Trans log frontier production function is written for three inputs—labor, capital, material, inputs and time in the following form, which is the extended version of equation (1):

$$\ln Y_i = \alpha_0 + \alpha_k \ln K_i + \alpha_l \ln L_i + \alpha_m \ln M_i + \varepsilon_{i,} \ldots\ldots\ldots\ldots\ldots\ldots (2)$$

where $\ln E_{i,} = \alpha + \varepsilon_{0i}$

α measures the mean efficiency level across firms and ε_{0i} measures the firm specific deviation from that mean (Hildreth and Houck, 1968). ε_{0i} is further decomposed into a predictable component V_i and a random component $U_{i,}$ resulting in the following equation:

$\ln Y_i = \alpha_i + \alpha_k K_i + \alpha_l \ln L_i + \alpha_i \ln M_i + V_{i+} U_i$....................

(3)

Where $\alpha_i + V_i = W_i$

This general production function allows undertaking different tests. The first test is to check whether intermediate inputs are separable from primary inputs or not.

The function signifies firm level productivity and U_i is a pure random element in production is representing unexpected deviations from the mean due to a host of exogenous factors. Estimation of total factor productivity (Using simple OLS) gives the equation:

$TFP_{it} = \widehat{w}_{it} = \hat{v}_{it} + \hat{\alpha}_0$

$= Y_i - \hat{\alpha}_0 - \hat{\alpha}_k \ln K_i - \tilde{\alpha}_l \ln L_i - \tilde{\alpha}_m \ln M_i$ ... ... (4)

According to Maddala (1977) firm level efficiency is then estimated as a residual of equation (4) by solving for ($\widehat{w}_i$) in level form efficiency represented as exp ($\widehat{w}_i$) residuals that is the productivity of the firm and denoted by TFP.

Adopting Ordinary Least Square (OLS) estimation method and technique, the research intends to measure the effects of bank credit on the levels of SMEs productivity over a given period. It investigates the extent to which the gap in total factor productivity between SMEs which use bank loan in the course of production process and the other group of SMEs only rely on internal source of funds.

This study estimates firm-level total factor productivity (TFP) as a residual from an augmented Cobb-Douglas production function and the methodology used are consistent with the methodology of Gatti and Love (2008) who calculated the potential output for the Bulgarian firm and assume the same specification of the Cobb-Douglas function for all countries with the mean input share.

In addition, this study also adopted different statistical techniques to estimate specified model results. Such as, the adjusted coefficient of determination (R-bar squared) was used to test the best-fit line and measures the explanatory power of the specified model (Nenadic and Zucchini, 2004). The '*t*-value' was used to determine the significance of the stated variables (Levinsohn and Petrin, 2000). The '*F*-Statistic' was also used to test the joint significance of the independent variables (Fadejeva and Melihous, 2009). It must be pointed out that in a cross section data analysis of this nature, the significance of the F-statistic is crucial as compared to the value of the R-bar squared.

Estimating Effect of Credit Access on Total Factor Productivity

The main objective was to estimate the effects of credit on SMEs total factor productivity. To capture the effect of credit on TFP, the following model was estimated;

$$\boldsymbol{TFP_i} = \gamma_i + \boldsymbol{\lambda_1 Credit_i} + \boldsymbol{\sigma X_i} + \upsilon_i \ldots\ldots\ldots\ldots\ldots\ldots\ldots\ldots\ldots\ldots \quad (5)$$

$$\mathbf{C_i} = \begin{cases} \textbf{1 if SME has to bank credit} \\ \textbf{0 if otherwise} \end{cases}$$

Where *TFPi* denotes TFP obtained from equation (4), Credit is a dummy variable equal to 1 if SMEs has access to credit and 0 if otherwise, and is a vector of control variables.

Potential Assumptions and Endogeneity

The required assumptions for the above multiple regression models are: (1) the error variable (ε) is normally distributed, (2) the mean value of the error variable is zero, (3) the variance of the error variable is a fixed but unknown value, (4) the values of the error variables are independent of one another, and (5) relationship between productivity and profitability with variables of bank credit is linear.

This study assumes SME's technological viability determines and limits the transformation of inputs into production possibilities and is denoted by Y. Through a given process, technology converts production inputs into outputs. The production possibility set is the set of all potential alternative production plans Y = (y1, y2...ym) and yi represent inputs and outputs of the plan. Hence, by applying Cobb-Douglas production function; this study econometrically examines the effect of bank credit on enterprises TFP.

In equations (5) the credit variables are potentially endogenous. This is because banks are more likely to lend to firms that are more productive. OLS estimates may therefore be biased. An effective way to test and overcome the potential endogeneity bias is the use of instrumental variables and two stage least square method (Ibarraran *et al.,* 2009). This method, however, also has a shortcoming due to difficulty in getting 'good instruments'. According to Du *et al* (2012), good instruments should be correlated with the endogenous explanatory variable and should only affect the dependent variable through the endogenous explanatory variable and not through any other channel. To check that for robustness of OLS estimates, this study will also use instrumental variables and two-stage least square.

4.8.2 ESTIMATION OF SME PROFITABILITY

This study looks at the extent to which bank credit has affected the profitability of Ethiopian manufacturing SMEs in a specific period. In accordance with related literature (Olutunla & Obamuyi, 2008) and models of firm's profitability (Margaret, 2003) the following equation states a linear, dynamic mathematical model of firm profitability. The equation specifies profitability as the dependent variable, and loans, sales, age of business, size of business and interest rate as independent variables. The equation measures the level of SMEs profitability on the basis of returns on investment and key measures of performance.

The fixed-effect regression model is specified as:

$$\pi = \mu_{jt} + \gamma_1 L_{jt} + \gamma_2 Sa_{jt} + \gamma_3 A_{jt} + \gamma_4 Si_{jt} + \gamma_5 I_{jt} + \varepsilon_{jt} \ldots\ldots\ldots$$

(Margaret, 2003)

Where, $\gamma_1 > 0; \gamma_2 > 0; \gamma_3 > 0; \gamma_4 > 0; \gamma_5 < 0$,

π is Profit, **Sa** is Sale, **L** is Loans, **A** is Age , **Si** is size , **I** is interest , ε_{jt} and μ_{jt} are intercepts coefficients and $\boldsymbol{\gamma_1}$; $\boldsymbol{\gamma_2}$; $\boldsymbol{\gamma_3}$; $\boldsymbol{\gamma_4}$; $\boldsymbol{\gamma_5}$ are parameters to be estimated.

Data measurement and Sources: Profit is measured by the amount of business return in terms of birr for firm j at time t, Loans are measured by the amount of bank credit obtained by firm j at time t. Sales are measured by the total amount of sales by firm j at time t. Age is measured by enterprise's years of business operation by firm j at time t, Enterprise Size measured by the number of employees at time t, interest rate is measured by Monetary Policy Rate (MPR). All the data, except interest rates are derived from the Ethiopian large and medium manufacturing enterprises survey data. The amount of interest rate for a given period is obtained from the National Bank of Ethiopia (NBE).

4.8.3 ORDINARY LEAST SQUARE ESTIMATION

To estimate the level of SME productivity and profitability with and without bank credit access, the study utilises regression analysis, specifically Ordinary Least Square (OLS) estimation model and can be used to estimate TFP and profitability of the given SMEs. To control the impact of input choice the study uses several estimates of TFP and profitability to check for robustness and minimise possible biases or errors.

4.9 RELIABILITY AND VALIDITY

Reliability is used to indicate 'the extent to which the different items, measures, or assessments are consistent with one another' and 'the extent to which each measure is free from measurement error' (Leech *et al*, 2005, p. 63). The primary purpose of reliability analysis is to analyse the internal consistency and reliability of each factor. Study reliability also relates to how data collections have been undertaken, type of instruments used to collect data can give consistent readings.

The study has taken important steps to ensure the CSA of Ethiopia manufacturing survey data is with good quality. This was done by ensuring the validity and reliability of the data used at various stages of the research process. Cleaning the data to minimize noise and produce a robust estimation is also one of the tasks that were done with care. At first, observations with missing values in either the value of production or one of the inputs are cleared from the data. Outliers are also controlled in the estimation in two ways. First, given each year's data, observations with extreme low values for any of the variables are cleared as they may highly influence the inefficiency of a given sector. These observations constitute about 2 percent of each year's data. Further, in some cases extreme values far from the large concentrations are cleared. The final data used for estimation are unbalanced panel data from the years 2005/06–2011/12.

In addition the study has considered and checked the validity of the data and instruments used to obtain the data by implementing the Hausman test. Regarding to the data Central Statistics Agency of Ethiopia is designed to exclude micro scale industries with fewer than 10 employees however, some enterprises in the survey data set reported fewer than 10 workers.This study has started compiling the survey data by removing this micro enterprises repeated (panel) observations, non-manufacturing enterprises, and observations with missing or incomplete data also removed. Moreover, the study checked for the presence of outliers using the share of labour in value added and the capital-value added ratio.

In line with the data reliability check the study go through the survey questionnaire (see Appendix E) and tried to cross check respondents answer. At the last the study tries to interact with the Ethiopian CSA colleagues who have participated on the data collection processes at different level and that has helped to resolve vague or unclear information. The number of observations per region, the year of data collection, and summary statistics for other key variables is presented in the Appendix D. This raw survey data has comprehensive source of information that this study want to collect and it has a kind of data that align with the focus of this study topic. Moreover, the survey data coverage is also nationwide, the data was collected by central statistical agency of Ethiopia, and then the source is reliable and highly credentials. The results of this study are likely to be reliable too.

4.10 ETHICS

According to Collis and Hussey (2009), the central ethical issues are related to voluntary participation, anonymity and confidentiality. This study followed the 'Code of Research Ethics of Tshwane University of Technology', which requires certain forms to be submitted to the Faculty of Management Science Research Ethics Committee for approval prior to the fieldwork. Accordingly, ethical clearance was sought from the University before commencing the study. It showed the title of the research, the researcher's details, the purpose of the research, what it involved and the voluntary nature of participation and confidentiality. The clearance letter is attached in Appendix E.

4.11 CONCLUSION

The research methodology for this study includes research design, variable definitions and measurements, model development, data collection methods, and data analysis. The chapter also discussed the key variables in the study and how the data collection instruments were designed and used. Further, the data analysis approach was discussed.

The following section (chapter 5) presents the descriptive findings of the research study, interprets significance of these findings, and presents the results of testing the model of SME productivity and profitability. It also explains how the model developed from the literature review and how it is supported by data analysis.

CHAPTER 5: DATA ANALYSIS

5.1 INTRODUCTION

This chapter presents the preliminary data analysis of the results of the study. This is composed of descriptive findings of key data variables, which are stated in two main sections. The first section describes the general SME characteristics, and the second section presents key data findings.

The next sections present descriptive data analysis results with respect to enterprise ownership, industry types, age group, and firm size and so on. Since all these variables may be associated with significant differences in characteristics and performances of SMEs.

5.2 DATASET DESCRIPTION

The study used manufacturing survey data and not interview because the data has all the necessary and comprehensive information for the thesis. The firm level panel survey data of manufacturing enterprises collected annually by Central Statistics Agency (CSA) of Ethiopia for the period 2005-2012. The annual surveys conducted by CSA covers all manufacturing establishments that employ at least 10 and more workers and use electricity in production. Information regarding costs of materials, number of employees, fixed capital, total wages paid, gross value of production, energy expenditure, among other issues is largely covered in the surveys.

Moreover, the dataset incorporates information on quantity and unit prices of the commodity products as well as investment and other industrial costs, sales, employment, depreciation and stock of capital, access to credit, access to output market (local and export), type of ownership, number of years in business and the conditions of accounting record keeping.

The variables *y* and *x* in the production function specified above are defined as vectors of outputs and inputs, respectively. Based on the data, the appropriate value that could represent *y* is either the gross value of production or value added (gross value of production net of raw materials and energy used in production). In this respect TFP can be calculated based on gross-output (gross-output based TFP) or value added (value added based TFP). Nagler and Naudé (2014) noted that for comparing TFP growth at the industry level, it is best to use value added output rather than gross output as the latter includes the purchase of intermediate inputs, which may vary greatly among industries.

Taking into account of the availability of data on sales, amount of credit, firm size, firm age, raw materials and energy, and importance of intermediate inputs in the production process, this study employed output based TFP analysis and linear dynamic model for the estimation of SMEs profitability.

While the dependent variable in the production functions (*y*) is the gross value of production (sales revenue), the vector of inputs includes labour (given by total wages and salaries), capital, costs of raw materials, and energy expenditure. Data on fixed capital are presented in the survey by including value of fixed assets at the beginning of the survey year, new capital expenditures, capital sold and disposed during the year, depreciation, and the book value at the end of the year. Thus, capital is measured by the net value of fixed assets at the end of the survey year. The other two inputs are raw materials and energy. Raw materials include expenditure on imported and domestic intermediate goods. Similarly, energy input includes expenditure on fuel, electricity, wood and charcoal used for production.

5.2.1 STUDY POPULATION AND SAMPLE SIZE

Manufacturing industry nationwide survey data, collected by the Central Statistical Agency (CSA) of Ethiopia from the years 2005 to 2012 covers a total observation of 2,682 manufacturing establishments employing ten persons and above. This study considers total manufacturing survey data observation (i.e. 2,682 enterprises) as a population. Out of the total observation, this study, only considers an employment level of more than 10 and less than 100 people. Hence, out of a total population of 2,682 only 1,542 enterprises are selected and used in the study.

Table 5.1: List of Manufacturing Industries in a given year

Years	Micro (0-9)	Small (10-20)	Medium (21-99)	Large (100^+)	Total
2005/06	2	404	136	207	749
2006/07	4	700	179	224	1,107
2007/08	3	881	165	236	1,285
2008/09	5	1,191	195	264	1,655
2009/10	44	1,264	193	274	1,775
2010/11	102	1,168	243	374	1,887
2011/12	35	1,253	242	332	1,862

Source: Own calculation based on data from CSA Manufacturing Survey (2005 - 2012)

Note 1: *This survey is designed to exclude small-scale industries with fewer than 10 employees however, some firms in the LMMIS data set reported fewer than 10 workers.*

Note 2: *These statistics do not capture changes in part-time employment or shifts in hiring from full-time to part-time employees.*

Table 5.1 indicates that the total number of manufacturing enterprises for the year 2005 was 749 and there was a growth in the number of enterprises over the years. For the year 2011, the total number of manufacturing enterprises grew to 1,862. This population size is before outliers. The actual number in regressions differs due to non-response key variables.

Table 5.2: Firm Size Transition in Manufacturing (t=2005-2012)

		Year t+1				
		Micro (0-9)	Small (10-20)	Medium (21-99)	Large (100^+)	
Year t	Small (10-20)	9.8%	78.9%	10.4%	0.9%	100%
	Medium (21-99)	1.5%	8.6%	84.5%	5.4%	100%

Source: Own calculation based on data from CSA Manufacturing Survey (2005 – 2012)

Table 5.3: Small and Medium (SMEs) manufacturing enterprises (Sample Size)

Years	Small (10-20)	Medium (21-99)	Total
2005/06	404	136	540
2006/07	700	179	879
2007/08	881	165	1046
2008/09	1,191	195	1386
2009/10	1,264	193	1457
2010/11	1,168	243	1411
2011/12	1,253	242	1495

Source: Own calculation based on data from CSA Manufacturing Survey (2005 - 2012)
Note: *This sample size is before outliers. Sample size in regressions differs due to nonresponse key variables.*

Table 5.3 shows the number of Small and Medium manufacturing enterprises from the years 2005 to 2012 and this list is the actual sample size for the study. The sample size survey data is designed to exclude micro and large manufacturing enterprises (excluded with fewer than 10 and more than 100 employees). This manufacturing data groups covered in this study are manufactures of food products, chemical and chemical products, rubber and plastic products, fabricated metal products (except machinery and equipment), beverages, non-metallic mineral products, textiles, publishing and printing, tanning and dressing, and wearing apparel. These categories largely dominate the manufacturing sector of Ethiopia by employment, production, and value added.

5.3 BARRIERS OF ENTERPRISE PERFORMANCE

The descriptive statistics in Table 5.4 illustrate that around 36 percent of the manufacturing industries reported a shortage of supply of raw materials as a primary reason for not working at full capacity. Obstacles

Table 5.4: Major operational problem faced by Ethiopian manufacturing SME in 2005-2011

Major Problems Faced by the Enterprise	% of all Enterprises	% of Enterprises with Bank credit	% of Enterprises with no Bank credit
Shortage of supply of raw materials	36	33	35
Getting market/customers	14.55	10.23	17.63
Shortage of working capital	7.27	6.53	7.81
Inconvenient working place	2.28	2.39	2.39
Government rules and regulation	3.23	2.82	3.53
No problems faced	3.82	3.88	3.78
others	28.73	35.27	24.06

Source: Author's calculation based on CSA Manufacturing survey data (2005 - 2012)

Of those who reported shortage of supply of raw materials as a major problem, more than 33 percent were from the group that have access to bank credit for operations, and 35 percent were from the other group who operate production without access to bank credit. About 15 percent of all manufacturing industries reported absence of demand for products as a second major reason for not working at full capacity, and of these, more than 10 percent was bank credit recipients and around 18 non-recipients. Of those that reported a shortage of working capital as a major operational problem, more than 6 percent were from the enterprises with access to bank credit, and around 8 percent from the non-recipient group. The results are consistent with prior studies, such as WB (2012); WB (2015), and Beck and Demirguc-Kunt (2006), who found that access to finance remains a top obstacle for SMEs. This implies that the SMEs that have been expected to be graduated and joined the medium and large scale are still hampered by many and intertwined problems like access to finance and others.

Table 5.5: Patterns in Raw Material Use and Sources

	Share of Raw Materials in Value of Sales (%)	% of Enterprises Importing Raw Materials
Enterprises with Bank credit	51.11	65.05
Enterprises without Bank credit	53.49	48.28

Source: Author's calculation from Ethiopia CSA Manufacturing survey data (2005 - 2012)

Table 5.5 explains the patterns in raw material use and sources of raw material for manufacturing enterprises in the years 2005-2012. The percentage share of raw materials in the value of sale for the enterprises with bank credit is more than 51 percent and about 54 percent for the other group. On the other side, the percentage of imported raw materials by enterprises with bank credit and without bank credit are 65 percent and 48 percent respectively. In general, the shortage of supply of raw materials is a key problem faced by both groups of SMEs; however, the extent of the problem is not the same.

5.3.1 AGE GROUP AND SIZE

The findings suggest that age of SMEs varied between 8 years and 106 years, averaging at 21.6 years, with a standard deviation of 14.8 years. 'Total permanent employees' was used to measure the size of business. The minimum size of businesses was one employee and the maximum size of businesses was of 4,454 employees. The average size of businesses was 74 employees and the standard deviation was 208 employees. However, this study concentrates on the size of business with more than 10 and less than 100 employees.

The relationship between SMEs age and credit-constrained status is weaker. There is no significant difference between the degree of credit-constraint and firm age. This result shows that age is not a significant factor in predicting the probability of obtaining credit for manufacturing firms. Furthermore, the analysis reveals that a robust set of significantly negative performance characteristics is associated with being credit-constrained. Some results contradicted empirical studies that had been done by Fluck *et al.* (1998); Newman (2010). These prior studies supported the argument that younger firms face hardship and more costs in accessing external financing from lenders because information asymmetry. Consequently, it is hypothetical existence of a positive relationship between firm's age and access to debt finance by SMEs. This implies that credit lenders find the older firms are less risky since the firms have earned a relatively good reputation over time and the lenders know most of the older firms. .

5.3.2 ACCESS TO BANK CREDIT BY INDUSTRY GROUP

Nine major manufacturing subsectors are covered by the survey:- Food & Beverages, Textiles and Foot Ware, Cement, Printing & Publishing, Iron & Still, Plastics & Rubbers,

Chemicals and Pharmaceuticals, Food & Beverages, Cement, Wood & Furniture jointly account for 67 percent of the total of enterprises surveyed while they contribute only 22 percent of total employment and 24 percent of total sales. These industries are dominated by many small enterprises. In addition, Pharmaceuticals account for the highest share of employment (19 percent) and sales (22 percent), but represent only 0.5% of the enterprises in the data. Similar patterns hold with Textiles & Footwear; these industries are dominated by a few big enterprises. However, it should be noted that the variable 'industry' is not included in the model because all the firms belonged to one industry. Based on the dataset the following descriptive results are obtained with respect to SME locational distribution.

- Thirty-six percent of the firms were concentrated in the capital, fifty-five percent distributed across the four biggest regions and seven percent in the less developed regions.
- Government owned only around nine percent of the firms; the rest owned privately or by cooperatives.
- Seventy percent of the firms were established after transition to market economy (1992/93).
- Only four percent of SMEs engaged in export, of which fifty six percent are from the Textiles subsector and twenty seven percent from Food and Beverages.

Based on the data set the following descriptive results obtained with respect to SME access to bank credit by size

- A close look at the distribution of bank credit across firm size approximated by sales shows that it is highly skewed to big firms. Seventy-three percent of enterprises in the third and fourth sales quintile had access to bank credit, whereas 67 percent of firms in the first and second sales quintile did not.

Based on the dataset the following descriptive results are obtained with respect to SMEs access to bank credit by industry group. The same pattern is observed with the distribution of loans/credit across industry groups. Industries dominated by a few medium firms have significantly better access to credit than industries with many small firms. Seventy-five percent of firms in Pharmaceuticals, Printing and Chemicals have access to bank credit, while they jointly account for only 10 percent of total number of enterprises versus 40 percent of total sales. Only 33 percent of firms in Food & Beverages, Wood & Furniture and Cement have access to bank credit, while they account for 67 percent of the total number of enterprises versus only 24 percent of sales. The results are again consistent with prior studies, such as WB, (2012); WB, (2015), and Beck and Demirguc-Kunt (2006), who also found that access to finance remains a top obstacle for SMEs regardless of the type of industry. The problem is more serious on the small enterprises than medium once.

5.3.3 TYPE OF OWNERSHIP

There were three types of ownership observed, namely private, public and co-operative. Table 5.6 summarises the number of observations over 2005-2012 period with respect to ownership.

Table 5.6: Percentage Share of Manufacturing Enterprises Establishment By Type of Ownership and Age

Size category	Ownership category	Age	Observations
Medium	Public	Young	58
		Old	255
	Private	Young	317
		Old	177
Small	Public	Young	18
		Old	55
	Private	Young	372

	Old	647

Source: Author's calculation based on data from CSA Manufacturing Census (2005 - 2012)

Only public and private or co-operative enterprises were used in the model because the third type, 'Public or private' had relatively few observations and could bias the results. By this method of classification, 67.4 percent are privately owned and 16.4 percent are public and 5.4 percent are public or private owned enterprises. In the sample, productivity measures of TFP, value-added per capital, labour productivity (measured by sales per employee) vary considerably across the four groups. Foreign firms have the highest TFP and value-added per capital, but only have the second highest sales per employee after private firms. Private firms have higher TFP, but marginally lower value-added per capital than collective firms. All enterprises were in the production and manufacturing industry. Because of no variation in the industry, the variable industry is not included in the model.

5.3.4 REGION

The regional distribution of manufacturing enterprises is highly skewed to the urban areas. Slightly more than 40 percent of total manufacturing enterprises, which were operating in the reference year, are located in Addis Ababa. Following Addis Ababa, Oromia, S.N.N.P., Amhara and Tigray Regional States accounted for 40.29 percent; 20.76 percent; 13.44 percent; 10.68 percent; 9.16 percent and 5.67 percent of the total establishments respectively.

There is a large difference in enterprises number and size across regions; respectively in urban areas such as Addis Ababa region have well above large enterprises observations found such as 38.29% of the total manufacturing enterprises established in Addis Ababa. However, in Tigray region only have 9.16% of manufacturing enterprises.

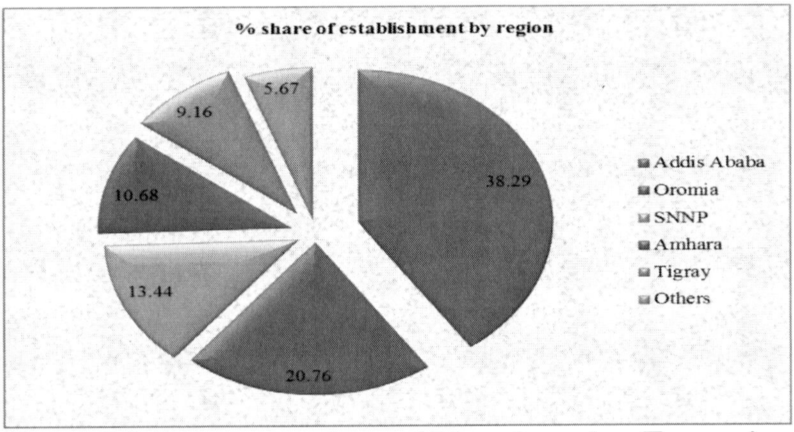

Figure 5.1: Percentage share of Manufacturing Enterprises by Region

Source: Author's calculation based on data from CSA Manufacturing Census (2005 - 2012)

In sum, banks tend to lend more to big enterprises. In terms of industry groups, this translated to greater access to industries with a few big enterprises and the opposite to industries with many small firms. In a well-functioning credit market, this should imply a higher-level efficiency among the big firms and whether this holds true is further investigated using an econometric analysis.

5.3.5 ENTERPRISES CASH FLOW STATUS

Before analysing SME profitability with respect to access to finance, first it is better to examine the enterprises level of cash flow. Then respectively this section examines enterprises characteristics associated with being financially constrained or not.

The previous studies conducted by Fazzari *et al,* (2000) revealed that the extent of enterprises financial constraints is correlated with their cash flow. The notion of this perception is that if enterprises are free in its access to external financing that means its investment patterns should not be correlated to its cash flows. On the opposite, the existence of credit constraints would lead to a situation where the firm is only able to invest in the presence of positive cash flows. Using this approach, this study tries to identify whether SMEs are credit-constrained or not using Ethiopian manufacturing industry survey data of a given period and tries to identify which types of firms are more likely to be credit-constrained.

The analysis revealed that investment choices and actions of manufacturing firms in Ethiopia highly rely on enterprises level of cash flows (see Table 5-7). This further confirms that enterprises are constrained in access to external financing sources when making investments in fixed assets such as machinery or the purchase of land. Moreover, the findings show that these credit constraints are stronger for young and small enterprises being more liquidity constrained than other group of enterprises. This findings support the previous studies (see Faulkender *et al.,* 2012; Barbi, 2012; Deakins *et al.,* 2008). Most of them secure loans for their businesses using the owner-managers' personal assets.

Table 5.7: Investment on cash flow – Manufacturing Enterprises

	1 Normalized investment	2 Normalized investment	3 Normalized investment
Cash Flow(CF)	0.0820*** (5.42)	0.0826* (2.24)	0.0527*** (4.23)
Cash Flow lagged	0.0134** (2.59)	0.0121 (0.71)	0.0137** (2.61)
Small	-0.0303 (-1.37)	-0.0696 (-0.89)	-0.0482* (-2.21)
Medium	-0.0223 (-1.20)	-0.0315 (-0.58)	0.0344 (-1.88)
Small x CF	-0.0640*** (-4.04)	-0.0717 (-1.54)	0.0391** (-2.78)

Medium x CF	-0.0415** (-2.86)	-0.0687 (-1.55)	-0.0240 (-1.76)
Young	-0.00795 (-0.57)	0.0657 (1.08)	-0.0112 (-0.79)
Young x CF	0.0164 (1.62)	0.0358 (1.02)	0.0238* (2.39)
Constant	0.0769**	-0.168	0.0904***
r2	0.0982	0.142	0.096
N	5958	1395	5882

Source: Authors calculation based on data from CSA Manufacturing Census (2005 - 2011)

Note 1: *All specifications include firm and year x industries fixed effects. Standard errors are listed in parentheses.* * *significant at 10%;* ** *significant at 5%;* *** *significant at 1%. All specifications include firm and year fixed x industries effects. Standard errors are listed in parentheses.*

Note 2: *Micro and Large enterprises are excluded from these model and firms are classified as small if the number of employees is between 10 and 19, medium if the number of employees is between 20 and 99. Firms are classified as young when they have been operating for less than or equal to 5 years.*

Fazzari *et al.* (2000) argue that credit-constrained firms have large costs of external financing and larger investments cash flow sensitivity than relatively unconstrained firms that have very small costs of external funds. Building on this approach this study tries to identify whether SMEs are credit-constrained or not. The findings show that investment decisions of manufacturing industry enterprises in Ethiopia is heavily dependent on cash flows. Accordingly, the above table suggest that in Ethiopian manufacturing enterprises cash flow is highly correlated with investment opportunities.

The table result confirms that manufacturing enterprises are constrained in access to external financing sources when making investments in fixed assets such as machinery or the purchase of land. This analysis also confirms that enterprises investment is challenged by liquidity constraints, and this implies that most investment decisions of manufacturing firms in Ethiopia are heavily dependent on cash flows or internal funds. This confirms that firms are constrained in access to external financing sources when making investments in fixed assets such as machinery or the purchase of land.

The findings further demonstrate that collateral requirements can be binding for smaller firms not to have credit access since, for the banks, the most common type of collateral used are land, buildings and personal assets. This confirms the views of previous studies, such as Fazzari *et al.* (2000), Almeida and Campello (2001), McMahon *et al.* (1993) and Almeida and Campello (2001) and firms' liquidity constraint theory developed by Myers & Rajan, 1998.

5.3.6 SME ACCESS TO BANK CREDIT BY SALES QUINTILE

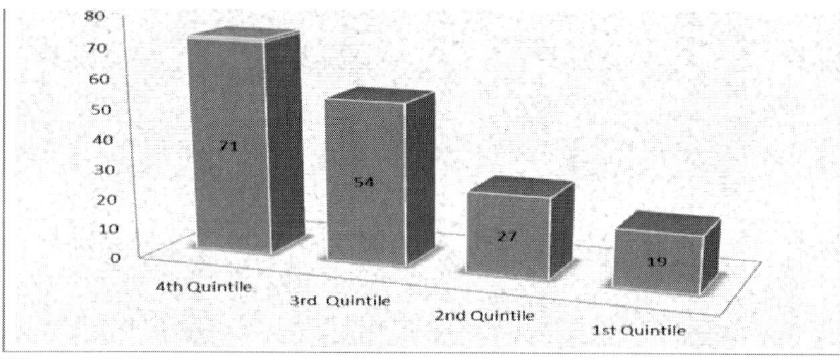

Figure 5.2: Percentage of Enterprises with Access to Bank credit by Sales Quintile

Source: Author's calculation based on data from CSA Manufacturing Census (2005 - 2012)

The analysis results show that the distribution of bank credit across firm size approximated by sales shows that it is highly skewed to big firms. Seventy three percent of enterprises in the third and fourth sales quintile had access to bank credit whereas sixty seven percent of firms in the first and second sales quintiles did not.

As illustrated in Figure 5.3 the set of indicators focusing on the use of financial services by big and small firms shows that in Ethiopia both big and small manufacturing enterprises rely on internal fund sources, however, in relative terms large enterprises use bank credit better than small enterprises. The results are consistent with prior studies, such as WB (2015), Beck *et al.* (2008), and Fuchs, (2011), who found positive associations between the size of enterprises and credit access.

The data analysis also presents the percentage of investment that is financed by different finance sources with respect to firm size. In Ethiopia manufacturing industry big firms have better experience in using an external source of finance like bank credit than small firms. The chart shows that there is an excessive reliance on internal funds by both big and small firms and is a sign of potentially inefficient financial intermediation in Ethiopia. The results also confirm the study of Kuntchev (2012) who establish that small enterprises prefer and mainly utilise internal sources of funds due to some obstacles while large enterprises have better chance in using external source of finance for their production process.

5.3.7 SME CONTRIBUTION

This section presents results of descriptive summaries of SMEs contribution in terms of value added and employment generation. The table below shows the outcomes for this particular analysis.

As shown in Table 5.8, in 2010 about 26 percent of total firms were engaged in food and beverage production and contributed about 33 percent and 35 percent of the total manufacturing sector's employment and value-added, respectively. Industries that might help accumulate technological capabilities and create dynamic inter-industry linkages, such as chemical, electrical and electronics, metal processing, and other engineering industries, are almost non-existent and the findings are much consistent with the previous study (Altenburg, 2010, p.115).

Table 5.8: Enterprises Contribution for Value-added and Employment

Industrial group	% of firms (of total no. of firms)		% share of value-added		% share of employment	
	2005/06	2009/10	2005/06	2009/10	2005/06	2009/10
Food and beverage	29.90	26.30	40.38	34.95	30.12	32.48
Non-metallic Minerals	12.20	22.20	15.70	19.24	8.52	10.53
Metal Products	8.50	7.00	3.04	6.93	6.68	5.78
Paper and paper products	7.00	5.66	5.35	4.89	6.81	5.40
Leather	5.06	5.24	4.37	2.34	1.79	2.17
Rubber and Plastic	5.00	6.40	8.87	7.38	5.83	7.49
Chemicals	4.30	4.40	4.86	8.10	4.79	6.04
Textiles	3.30	1.85	3.41	6.26	18.66	11.55
Others	23.34	19.15	10.1	8.42	11.9	13.17

Source: Compiled from Ethiopian Manufacturing Industry Survey data (2005–2012).

5.4 TRENDS OF SME PRODUCTIVITY AND PROFITABILITY

Figure 5.3 shows the graphs of the total factor productivity with respect to time range. The total productivity of Ethiopian manufacturing enterprises at any arbitrary year Y_0 corresponds to the slope of a ray drawn from the origin to the point along the total factor productivity. There is a decreasing trend of enterprise output over time especially from a year 2005 until 2007. The reason for this is not investigated in this paper. This model is used to predict output and therefore used to calculate productivity. For example, the trend of TFP is such that it steadily decreased between years 2005 and 2007 and then sharply increased thereafter.The figure also presents the level of manufacturing enterprises total factor productivity at year 2007 that is 0 after that until 2011 enterprises total factor productivity is measured below zero. The lowest enterprises total factor productivity observed in year 2009 and that measure is much below zero. However, the growth of total factor productivity is very sharply after 2009. There is a decreasing trend of enterprise output over time. The reason for this is not investigated in this paper. This model is used to predict output and therefore used to calculate productivity.

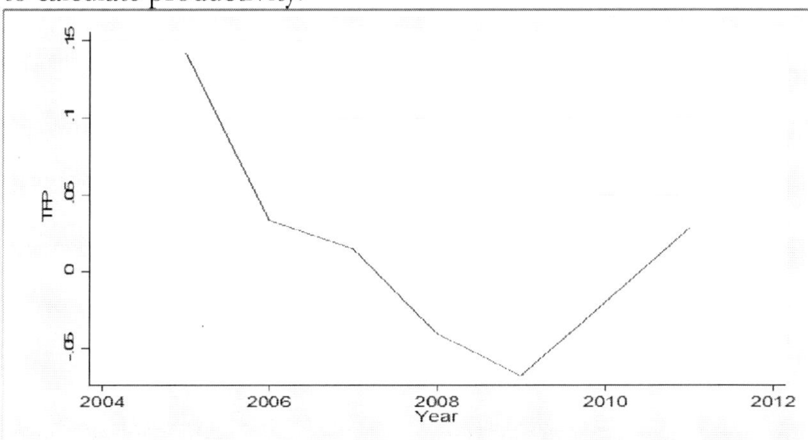

Figure 5.3: The trend of enterprises TFP (total factor productivity)

Source: Author's calculation based on data from CSA Manufacturing Survey (2005 - 2012)

Figure 5.4 presents the time trend of profitability performance of Ethiopian manufacturing enterprises for the given period. There are a number of important points or observations to be noted in this figure. Firstly, the figure shows that profitability of manufacturing enterprises in Ethiopia had a decreasing trend between years 2004 and 2008, then a sharp increasing thereafter. The graph also illustrates more or less constant average positive profit growth trend between years 2005 and 2007.

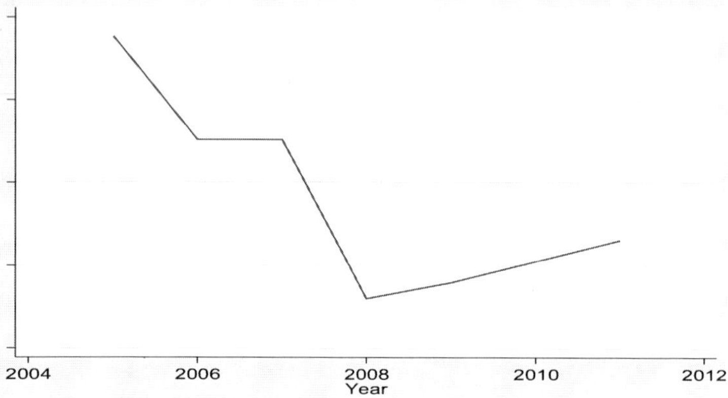

Figure 5.4: Trends for SME profitability performance over the period of 2005-2011
Source: Author's analysis (Profit and years) based on survey data from CSA (2005- 2011)

5.5 SUMMARY OF GENERAL DATA FINDINGS

About 68 percent of enterprises without access to bank credit during the period did not have proper accounting records compared to just 29 percent among enterprises with access. Given the poor conditions of information infrastructure in the country, banks may depend more on relationships in lending in general. However, the enterprises without access to bank credit might have been further disadvantaged given their comparatively shorter age on average; 35 percent with more than 15 years in business compared to 54 percent in the group with access to credit.

According to SMEs, owners' perspective the survey data reveals that bank-lending practice is characterised by highly collateralised lending - in some case banks require a collateral worth up to 80 percent of the value of the credit. Commercial banks are legally required to make 100 percent provision against bad credit without collateral and 50 percent provision for doubtful loans. Highly collateralised and relationship-based lending has thus far provided banks with a very little incentive for information based lending.

5.6 CONCLUSION

This chapter provides information on the survey data that this study used. This helps to understanding the existing situations of Ethiopian manufacturing enterprises with respect to finance access in a given year. An understanding of this background set can pave a way for further analysis of exploring the importance of bank credit and its impact on SME performance. Overall, the characteristics of the raw survey data reflect SMEs in the sample were found to be credit-constrained. This result is obtained by conducting liquidity constraint analysis. Moreover, this chapter graphically illustrated that the profitability and productivity of manufacturing enterprises in Ethiopia had a decreasing trend between years 2004 and 2008.

The next chapter seeks to test the psychometric properties of the extended model of estimation of SMEs productivity and profitability. This test helps estimate the extent of bank credit effect on enterprises productivity and profitability. Therefore, the next chapter presents the empirical results of the main research goals that relate to the effects of credit and SMEs performance.

CHAPTER 6: CREDIT ACCESS AND SME PERFORMANCE

6.1 INTRODUCTION

This chapter is organised into sections and subsections as the other parts of the thesis. Firstly, it presents regression results for estimating SME Total Factor Productivity (TFP). Secondly, this is followed by the presentation of results on bank credit access and SMEs productivity. SME TFP and are analysed by comparing the two SME groups. First group represents SMEs operating with access to finance and the other group belongs to SME operate without access to bank credit. This includes examining the effects of bank credit access and evaluating the role played by bank credit in SMEs performance in terms of TFP. This is followed by a discussion on the results of the regression analysis, TFP comparison between loan recipient and non-recipient groups of enterprises. The final section of this chapter presents the effects of bank credit on SMEs profitability and the results and conclusions.

6.2 ESTIMATION OF TOTAL FACTOR PRODUCTIVITY

The lagged production function specified and presented in question 3 in chapter 4 for a given three input variables was estimated by Ordinary Least Square (OLS) estimation method.

This helps to obtain the coefficients for labour, capital and material inputs. Accordingly, this analysis is done using three different models to estimate and calculate SME total factor productivity depending on the specification of the production inputs. The adopted fixed effect Models named as Model 1, 2 and 3, respectively. For each respective model OLS estimation techniques has been applied. The first model (model-1) is a basic model where the input-output variables are directly applied to the production function. The second model (model-2) is based where material inputs and capital are lumped together. The third model (model-3) introduces a host of control variables.

6.2.1 MODEL 1 REGRESSION ANALYSIS

In model 1, the input-output variables are directly applied to the production function and each pair of the three variables is linked separately to estimate SMEs productivity. The detailed econometric results are presented in appendix D (Table D.1). The results show that from a given enterprise, as the log of capital varies across time by one unit, the log of its output increases by .02 units holding other factors constant. As the log of the value of the wage total varies across time by one unit, the log of its output increases by .185 units holding other factors constant. The log of the value of raw materials varies across time by one unit, the log of its output increases by .717 units holding other factors constant.

As presented in the regression results in appendix D (Table D.1), the *p*-values of a major production inputs such as capital, labour and raw material inputs are 0.00. This further reveals that the F-value of 5871.67 with a p value of 0.00 significance at 1% indicate that the overall regression model is significant, hence, the joint contribution of the independent variables was significant in predicting the SMEs total factor productivity. It also suggests that the explanatory powers of overall models are adequate (Myers, 1990). This implies that *p*-value of capital is (p = 0.000<.01), means a one-point increase on capital; SMEs output will increase by 0.023 times. Similarly, the p value of labour (p = 0.000<.01) means a one-unit increase on labour; SMEs output will increase by 0.185 times and it is found to be highly significant ($p \leq 0.05$) and the correlation coefficient carries the expected positive sign. In addition p value of raw materials (p = 0.000<.01) are highly significant at the 1% significance level and affect productivity positively. That means a one-unit increase on material input; SMEs output will increase by 0.716 times.

Significant and positive coefficient for these inputs implies that enterprise productivity is serially correlated with the main production inputs and these inputs positively affect enterprises productivity. The results are consistent with prior studies, such as Gatti and Love (2006); Babajid (2012); Alfaro *et al.* (2009); Ang & Mckibbini (2006); Zhenhui & Sudeshna (2011); Nichter and Goldmark (2009) who also found statistically significant and positive relationship between total factor productivity growth and main factors of inputs like labour, capital and material inputs. The findings also support the Piketty's explanation of the increasing capital share in terms of marginal productivity theory. Marginal productivity theory proposes that a physical relation between quantities of inputs and a quantity of output, without prices; it is a technical relation, like an industrial engineering plan.

6.2.2 MODEL 2 AND REGRESSION ANALYSIS

In model 2, raw materials and capital are lumped together to the production process. The detailed econometric result is shown in Appendix D (Table D.2) and it is aligned with the findings obtained from model one... According to the results, the effect of the lumped inputs variable shows 0 p-values (p=.000<.01) and affect productivity positively. This shows that, as the log of the value of the lumped inputs varies across time by one unit, the log of its output increases by .762 units holding other factors constant, and all years are highly significant at the 1% level. This implies that, regression results the direct effect of overall production inputs lumped together on SMEs output is statistically significant (Lamped inputs =0.762, *p=0. 000* <0.001). The interesting finding is that the coefficients of the year dummies are negative. The cause and the reason behind this are apparently not clear in this study and it is beyond the scope.

6.2.3 MODEL 3 AND REGRESSION ANALYSIS

In Model 3, a host of control variables are introduced as independent variables; output, capital, labour, raw materials, time-fixed effects, age of business, type of ownership, size of business, industry, while Region 1 is used as the reference region. The other variables were introduced to control for the effect of enterprise specific factors like age, size and so on. It should be noted that variable "industry" is not included in the model because all the firms belonged to one industry such as the manufacturing industry. The detailed econometric result is shown in appendix D (Table D. 3 & 4). Time-effects dummies were created and included in the model, depicted in Appendix D. From this particular model, the following results were obtained:

The *p*-values of a major production inputs such as *p*-values of capital (p =0.000<.01), *p*-values of labour (p = 0.000<.01) and *p*-values of raw materials (p = 0.000<.01) are highly significant at the 1% significance level and affect productivity positively and all the years are highly significant, so they affect output. All independent variables except age affect output positively. According to the results, *p*-values of owner type (*p*-value =0.300>.10), *p*-values of size of business (p =0.978>.10) and *p*-values of region (p ranging from 0.231 to 0.978) are not significant even at 10% significant level. Therefore, these independent variables do not affect enterprise output. When the time effects are excluded, the following results are obtained and the detailed econometric result is shown in Appendix D. table A 15. It should be noted that when the time fixed effects were removed from the model, the age coefficient became highly significant (Prob. =.003<.01). The statistically significant negative relationship between SMEs output and age confirms the findings of Newman (2010); Vos *et al.* (2007); Rocca *et al.* (2009). On the other hand, the positive relationship between total factor productivity growth and main factors of inputs like labour, capital and material inputs and the use of other dummy variables is in line with prior studies (e.g. Van der Wijst, 1989; Daskalakis, 2008; Michaelas *et al.,* 1999; Cassar, 2004).

The summary of the three SME productivity-measuring models results are presented on Table 6.1 below. It shows that the overall models estimate statistically significant coefficients on major input items (L, K, and M) strongly and positively affect SME productivity. Most importantly, the models predict a similar pattern in factor elasticity across the two groups of enterprises namely bank credit users and non-users for their production process. More precisely, on the three different fixed-effect production regression model results found that p-values of capital (p =.002<.01), p-values of labour (p = 0.000) and p-values of raw materials (p =.000<.01) affect the production of an enterprise.

Table 6.1: Production function using capital, labour, raw materials, and time effect

Output	Coef.	Std. Err.	t	P>|t|	[95% Conf.	Interval]
ln_capital	.018	.0057	3.12	0.002	.0067	.0292
ln_wage	.116	.0205	5.63	0.000	.0754	.1559
ln_material	.701	.0273	25.71	0.000	.6477	.7545
2006/7	-.106	.0173	-6.12	0.000	-.1398	-.0720
2007/8	-.110	.0184	-6.01	0.000	-.1463	-.0743
2008/9	-.197	.0196	-10.08	0.000	-.2358	-.1590
2009/10	-.116	.0195	-5.92	0.000	-.1538	-.0772
2011/12	-.321	.0358	-8.95	0.000	-.3911	-.2506
Constant	**3.183**	**.3477**	**9.15**	**0.000**	**2.5010**	**3.8647**

Source: Author's calculation based on data from CSA Manufacturing Census (2005 - 2012)

This implies that enterprise, as the log of capital varies across time by one unit, the log of its output increases by .018 units holding other factors constant. As the log of the value of the wage total varies across time by one unit, the log of its output increases by .116 units holding other factors constant. The log of the value of raw materials varies across time by one unit, the log of its output increases by .701 units, holding other factors constant. The results indicate cross-sectional dependence and so heteroscedasticity in the data. The "frees" test is not performed due to having insufficient observations. In order to counteract the effect of the dependence, robust standard errors were used to estimate the regression model as follows.

Given a production function where the coefficients on inputs are estimated statistically significantly and consistently across different specifications, in the next sections the study can now precede with a discussion of the TFP estimated as a residual of the function.

6.3 ESTIMATED TFP BY ACCESS TO BANK CREDIT

The main research question for this study was whether bank credit merely has an effect on enterprise performance and to what extent it has an impact on SME productivity and profitability. The study attempted to answer this question by investigating and comparing TFP and rate of return on main production inputs across a sample of local manufacturing SMEs with and without access to bank credit. SME TFP (total factor productivity) with and without access to bank credit during the survey years are analysed and it is calculated by subtracting estimated enterprise output from the actual output. The study considers the empirical work done by Butler and Cornaggia (2007) on the relation between access to finance and firms productivity at the county level.

6.3.1 COMPARING GRAPHES

Figure 6.1 below shows that, for SMEs operating without bank loan, TFP has a decreasing trend between 2005 and 2008 and then a slight increasing trend thereafter, whereas for SMEs operating its production process with bank loan, TFP has a more gradual decreasing trend between 2005 and 2009 and then a sharp increasing trend thereafter. The graph illustrates that in a given specific time period TFP of enterprises operating there production without bank credit is slightly lower than SMEs operating there production process with access to bank credit. The graph has the tendency to not undermine the motivation and incentive of access to bank credit to SMEs that helps to be innovative improves their productivity performance.

Figure 6.1: Comparison of trends for companies operating with and without a bank credit

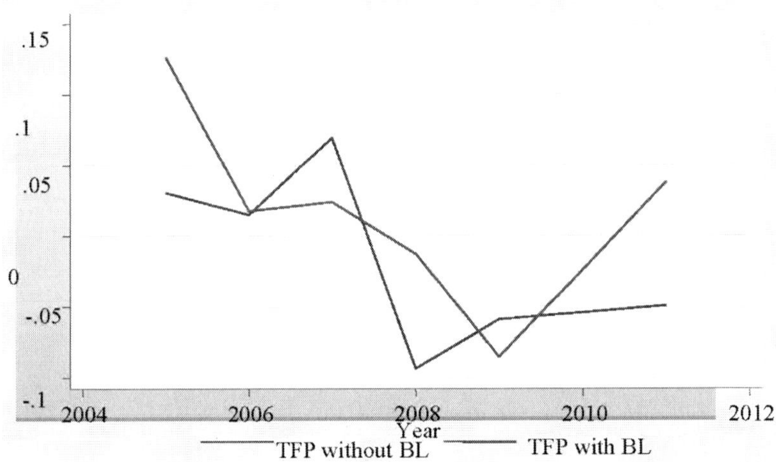

Source: Ethiopian CSA of manufacturing survey data of 2005-2012, and author's calculations
Note: TFP without BL = TFP without a bank credit; TFP with BL = TFP with a bank credit

Figure 6.2, below illustrates the average TFP among enterprises that operate with access to bank credit is 1.18 times higher in the second input output estimation model. Moreover, the differences in means are statistically significant across all the models. The same pattern holds when the basic model is estimated for the three biggest (Pharmaceuticals, Printing and Chemicals) vs. the three smallest industry groups (Food & Beverages, Cement and Wood & Furniture).

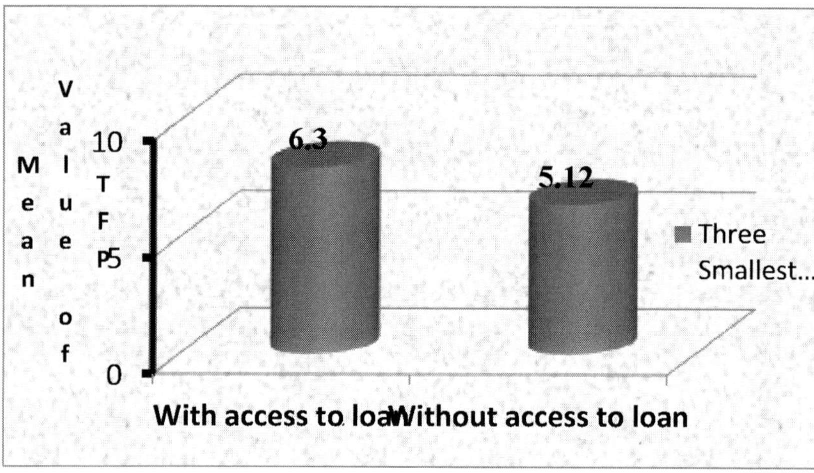

Figure 6.2: TFP of enterprises with and without bank credit

Source: Ethiopian CSA of manufacturing survey data of 2005-2012, and author's calculations

Figure 6.3 also indicates that the mean of TFP values for SMEs with access to bank credit is slightly higher than that of SMEs that are "not efficient" in access to credit for the three respective models. This result is empirical evidence to demonstrate to SMEs that enterprises should pay more attention to securing access to bank credit if they want to improve productivity and survive in the uncertain business environment in Ethiopia.

A value of variable (Yes) was given to an enterprises that had access to credit and (No) to an enterprises that had no access to credit from banks at least in the given survey years. By emphasising, the importance of access to bank credit practices on SME productivity the hypothesis of difference in mean of TFP of the two SME groups is tested. Respectively the Ordinary Least Squares (OLS) technique was used in estimating the specified econometric model. Since, apart from its simplicity, Ordinary Least Squares (OLS) technique gives reliable estimates (Fadejeva and Melihous, 2009).

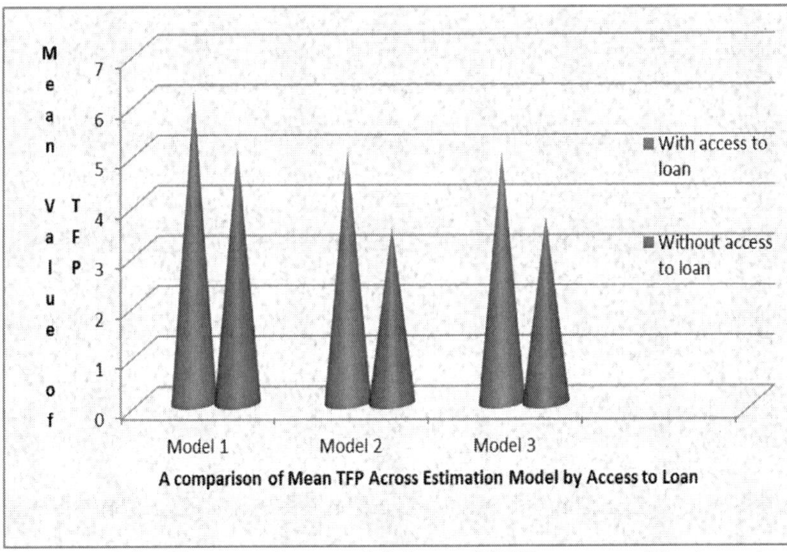

Figure 6.3: Comparison of Mean TFP across Estimation Model by Access to loan

Source: Ethiopian CSA of manufacturing survey data of 2005-2012, and author's calculations

6.3.2 COMPARING COEFFICIENTS ON INPUTS

The coefficients obtained from the estimation of SME TFP using a Cobb-Douglas production function for the two SME groups. The results show the responsiveness of sales or outputs to changes in the levels of each input used in production processes. Contrary to the estimation of the production function in all the three models explained above in a general sense, this section provides detail statistical results for the three models again for both credit recipients and non-recipient SME groups.

Table 6.2: produces and summarizes findings from all the three respective regression estimation models for each (credit recipient and non-recipient) group of enterprises. The results also indicate that among 1,542 total sample SMEs, 689 of them were credit recipients and the rest 856 were non- recipient SMEs. These results confirm previous studies (see World Bank, 2015; Kuntchev *et al.*, 2012) that majority of the SMEs from developing countries do not have access to credit and over half of SMEs are credit constrained in the Sub-Saharan Africa (SSA) region. Which is higher than in any other region. Such findings support the pecking order theory that proposes that firms will only seek external finance when they have exhausted all sources of internal finance.

From the table 6.2 below the significantly positive coefficient of production inputs for lagged productivity for both groups of enterprises implies that firms' productivity is serially correlated with factors of inputs. This input coefficients called output elasticity of a given input and is derived from the partial derivative of the logged value of output with respect to the logged value of respective input (Inomata, 2008). Most importantly all three models predict a similar pattern in factor elasticity across the two groups of enterprises (see Table 6.2 below for a detailed summary report on the econometric results).

In other words, an increase in enterprises total factor productivity (TFP) is an increase in the overall productivity (efficiency) of the enterprises. Since more output can now be produced than earlier, with each of the factors of production remaining the same. The present study results presented on table 6.2 consistent with the previous research findings (i.e. Lashitew, 2011, Nichter and Goldmark, 2009). It indicates the findings related with output elasticity or the returns to scale which is the sum of output elasticity with respect to each input used in the production function for both groups of enterprises. The results also shows that Ethiopian manufacturing enterprises (be credit recipient or non-recipients) have high and significant output elasticity with respect to material inputs followed by a relatively lower but significant elasticity with respect to labour and capital. The monotonicity principle of production implies that increase in input must not result in deterioration of output and the elasticity must be positive (Chatzikokolakis and Martin, 2008). However, according to Hepburn and Baptist (2012) high output elasticity of intermediate inputs is not a good indicator for the sector since; it implies that the sector may not use existing factors of inputs efficiently. This may imply that the manufacturing enterprises sector has lower value added and/or is heavily dependent on raw materials (ibid). The lower output elasticity with respect to capital than material inputs is an indication that the Ethiopian manufacturing sector is less responsive to changes in capital accumulation. These results confirm previous studies (see Abegaz, 2013) and it could arise from capital intensive technologies (use of large or more machineries and equipment) or use of older techniques of production (Demeke *et al.*, 2006).

Table 6.2: Production function using capital, labour, raw materials, energy and other industrial inputs

Variables (TFP)	1 Coefficients (with credit)	2 Coefficient (without credit)
ln_wage_{t-1}	0.245**	0.193***
	(10.67)	(10.91)
$ln\_capital_{t-1}$	0.0399***	0.0642***
	(4.62)	(6.43)
$ln\_material_{t-1}$	0.508***	0.598***
	(45.21)	(44.72)

ln_energy_{t-1}	0.0592***	0.0881***
	(5.71)	(6.50)
$ln\_other{\sim}st_{t-1}$	0.0562***	0.0410***
	(5.43)	(3.92)
_cons	1.512***	2.020***
	(10.99)	(14.31)
N	689	853
R-sq.	0.963	0.943

Source: Author's calculation based on data from CSA Manufacturing Census (2005 - 2012)

t statistics in parentheses. * $p<0.05$, ** $p<0.01$, *** $p<0.001$

As summarized in Table 6.2 above, raw materials and labour inputs have the highest elasticity in both credit recipient and non-recipient SME groups. In the basic and in the third models, a 100 percent increase in the value of capital is predicted in a 6.4 percent increase in the value of output of enterprises with no access to credit. This is 4.6 percent in those enterprises with access to credit (on average and holding other inputs constant), and a 100 percent increase in the value of labour is predicted to result in a 10.9 percent increase in the value of output of enterprises with no access to credit. While this is 10.7 percent in the group with access to credit. Similarly, a 100 percent increase in the value of material input is predicted to result in a 44.7 percent increase in the value of output of enterprises with no access to credit and 45 percent in the other group.

The average elasticity values across the two groups are 0.45 for material input, 0.11 for labour, 0.055 for capital, 0.06 for energy input and 0.042 for other related production inputs. For enterprises operating without bank credit, the average elasticity values across the two groups are 0.6 for material input, 0.2 for labour, 0.04 for capital, 0.07 for energy input and 0.06 for other related production inputs respectively. These numerical results indicates that Ethiopian manufacturing enterprises have high and significant output elasticity with respect to material inputs followed by labour irrespective of the different groups.

On the other hand the coefficients of total factor productivity inputs presented in the table 6.2 are all positive and significant. Since the dependent variable such as total factor productivity is log-transformed and the independent variable is in levels, the coefficient can be modified to give the percentage change for productivity that result from a unit change in the independent variables. Important to note that access to independent variables like labour measured as the proportion of the number of employees, the result indicates that increasing labour by one unit increase SME productivity by 10.7 in credit recipient firm and 11 by non-recipient firms. This would imply that increasing the proportion of labour by one percent would increase firms' productivity by around 11 percent for credit recipient and 10.7 percent for the other group.

An important observation from the above table is; relative elasticity of capital is low compared to other main production inputs for the two groups. This may imply that the sector has heavily dependent on material inputs and produce lower value added and low in employment generation. This finding is complements previous empirical works done in Ethiopian manufacturing sector (see Abegaz, 2013; Gebreeyesus, 2008; World Bank; 2014; World Bank, 2011). Those studies argue that the contributions of manufacturing sector in sub-Saharan Africa particularly Ethiopia is still insignificant and unsatisfactory. In both models 1 and 2 the share of capital is lowest in the SMEs operating with access to bank credit compared to enterprises operating without bank credit. This means that more capital is used in the production process of enterprises operating with bank loan than the other group.

Table 6.3: Production function using 1st (basic) model with capital and raw material lumped together

Variables (TFP)	Coefficients (with credit)	Coefficient (without credit)

ln_waget-1	0.169**	0.133***
	(9.13)	(9.22)
ln_capitalt-1	0.0604***	0.0638***
	(31.90)	(38.31)
ln_energyt-1	0.0989**	0.080**
	(1.96)	(2.33)
ln_other~st-1	0.1638***	0.1129***
	(3.82)	(4.52)
_cons	1.021***	0. 511***
	(5.16)	(11.36)
N	689	853
R-sq.	0.963	0.943

Source: Author's calculation based on data from CSA Manufacturing Census (2005 - 2012)

t statistics in parentheses; * $p<0.05$, ** $p<0.01$, *** $p<0.001$

The other important finding from the above table is; for each group of enterprises, the sum of the five-factor elasticity is around 1. This corresponds to the assumption of the Cobb-Douglas production function. The input factor elasticity obtained from the estimation yields comparable results to several other studies.

From the multiple regressions results presented above in table 6.3 labour inputs is not statistically significant at 10% confidence level even if the coefficient is positive. This indicates that there is positive relationship between Total Factor Productivity (TFP) of SMEs even if the impact is not significant. This means that, other things being equal, as the number of employee increases by one unit, TFP of SMEs also increases by 9.22 for enterprises with bank loan and 9.13 for the other group. However, that impact is not significant.

On the other hand, capital is significant at 10% and it has a positive relationship with TFP of SMEs for the two groups. This means that as capital increases by one unit, the enterprises' TFP also grow by 31.90 for credit recipient SMEs and 38.31 for the other groups. In addition, material input is not significant at 1% confidence level however; the coefficient is positively related with SMEs TFP. This means that when material input increases by a unit TFP of SMEs also increases by 44.72 for credit recipients SMEs while 45.21 for non-recipient group.

To sum up this section, considering the independent variables, labour, capital and material inputs for the two enterprise groups all have positive relationship with TFP of the SMEs and therefore contributed to the performance of SMEs in Ethiopia. The positive relationship between SMEs total factor productivity and main factors of inputs like labour, capital and material inputs is in line with prior studies (e.g. Bartelsman *et al.*, 2000; Cressy, 1995; Michaelas et al., 1999; Cassar, 2004).

The estimated result of R-Squared presented in the above two tables (table 6.2 and 6.3) showed that R-Squared of 0.963 for credit recipient SMEs and 0.943 non-recipient SMEs. This indicates that 96% of the variations in the TFP of SMEs are explained by the independent variables for first group of SMEs and 94% for the second group. This percentage shows a good fit of the model. The F-Statistic which is a key statistic in this cross-section study is 2.0033 (0.048) and is significant at 95% confident level. This implies that almost all the independent variables in the model have jointly contributed to the TFP performance of the SMEs in Ethiopia.

6.4 T-test on DIFFERENCE IN MEAN OF TFP

This section is a key point for the main contributions of the study because the analysis is directly in line with access to credit. Accordingly, with the objective of emphasising the importance of access to bank credit on SMEs productivity, the difference in mean of TFP of the two SME groups is tested and the results are presented in Table 6.4 and 6.5 below. A value of variable (Yes) was given to an enterprise that had access to credit and (No) to an enterprise that had no access to credit from banks at least for the given survey years. In the study availability of credit for SMEs from the bank for the given period of time is considered and those SMEs that have access to credit from banks are expected to improve their productivity performance.

The results presented in table 6.4, and table 6.5 below indicate that average TFP among enterprises with access to bank credit is 1.25 times higher in the first and second input output estimation model, while 1.08 times higher in the third input output estimation model. This econometric estimates result further indicates that, over the analysed period, access to bank credit affected the productivity growth of Ethiopian SMEs. This effect is evident in the positive coefficient for major productivity inputs and differences in mean of TFP of the two groups. In general, the average TFP among enterprises with access to bank credit is slightly higher than non-credit recipient enterprises.

This implies that TFP growth is sensitive to access to bank credit. This finding further implies that in Ethiopia SMEs' TFP growth is constrained by the availability of external funds. The results are consistent with prior studies, such as Gatti & Love (2006), Love (2003), Butler & Cornaggia (2007), Badia & Slootmaekers, (2008), Lashitew (2011), Emecheta & Ibe (2014) who found positive associations between coefficients for major productivity inputs and attribute large productivity improvements to access to bank credit. The results also confirm the study of Miller (1998) who argued that financial market development contributes to economic growth as well as firm's productivity improvement. Well-developed financial systems ease external financing constraints facing firms, which illuminate one mechanism through which financial development influences productivity improvement.

The next step is to check whether this TFP differences means for the two groups of SMEs are statistically significant across all the models or not. The significance level of the results can be estimated through hypothesis testing.

Table 6.4: T-test on difference in mean value of TFP across enterprises with and without Bank credit for 1st and 2nd model

Variable	Obs	Mean	Std. Err	Std. Dev	[95% Conf. Interval]	
Yes	689	6.29	.210	7.66	7.79	8.85
No	853	5.04	.157	3.85	4.84	5.45
combined	1542	6.97	.174	6.52	6.63	7.31
diff		1.25	.067	3.81	1.95	3.40

Source: Author's calculation based on data from CSA Manufacturing Census (2005 - 2012)
diff = mean (yes) - mean (no) t = 1.25 (difference in mean value of TFP across enterprises with and without access to bank credit) Pr (T < t) = 1.00 Pr (|T| > |t|) = 0.0000 Pr (T > t) = 0.00
Ha: diff < 0 Ha: diff! = 0 Ha: diff > 0 and Ho: diff = 0
Satterthwaite's degrees of freedom = 1118.94
Note 2: *Micro firms are excluded from these models. Firms are classified as small if the number of employees is between 10 and 19, medium if the number of employees is between 20 and 99, and large is the number of employees is above 100. Firms are classified as young when they have been operating for less than 5 years (or equal). Firms are classified as young when they have been operating for less than 10 years (or equal).*

Table 6.5: T-test on difference in mean TFP across enterprises with and without access to bank credit for 3rd model

variable	obs	Mean	Std. Err	Std. Dev	[95% Conf. Interval]	
Yes	689	4.23	.13	3.754	6.51	7.03
no	853	3.15	.06	1.473	3.03	3.27
combined	1542	3.93	.09	2.497	4.35	5.421

diff	1.08	.07	3.47	3.76

Source: Author's calculation based on data from CSA Manufacturing Census (2005 - 2012)
diff = mean (no) - mean (yes) t = 24.9597 Pr (T < t) = 1.00 Pr (|T| > |t|) = 0.00 Pr (T > t) = 0.00 Ha: diff < 0 Ha: diff! = 0 Ha: diff > 0 Ho: diff = 0, Satterthwaite's degrees of freedom =1118.94.

6.4.1 HYPOTHESIS TESTING

This section presents the results of T-test difference on mean values to test the study null (H_0) and alternative hypothesis (H_1) as presented in chapter 4. It is much more common for a research to be interested in the difference between means than in the specific values of the means themselves. The remarkable observations for the study from t-test on the difference in mean values of TFP across enterprises with and without access to bank credit exhibits slightly higher average TFP among credit recipient SMEs than the other group (see Table 6.4 & 6.5). More specifically, the regression results indicate that average TFP among enterprises with access to bank credit is 1.25 times higher in model 1 and in model 2 presented in tables 6.4 and 1.08 times higher in model 3 presented in tables 6.5.

In addition the above table 6.4 shows that the mean values of SME's with bank credit (1st group) is 6.29 and the mean value of SME's without bank credit (2nd. group) is 5.04 and the two groups of SMEs have different standard errors, equal to 0.210 and 0.157 respectively. The study considers the 95 percent confidence interval for the difference between the two groups of SMEs mean values and calculates the 95 percent confidence interval. The root of the discrepancy is that distance from the mean is calculated in a different way for the t-statistic than it is for mean confidence intervals (Boland, 2000). Notice that mean confidence interval bounds are based on the magnitude of the respective groups of SME standard errors (SE_1, SE_2). To conduct the hypothesis testing the study considered three important conditions.

1. The means are significantly different when: $\mu_1 - \mu_2 > 1.96\sqrt{SE_1^{\,2} + SE_2^{\,2}}$ ....Boland, (2000)
2. There is no overlap between confidence interval when: $\mu_1 - \mu_2 > 1.96\sqrt{SE_1 + SE_2}$ ....Dixon and Massey (1983)
3. The square root of the sum of squares of two numbers is less than the sum of those numbers, $\sqrt{SE_1^{\,2} + SE_2^{\,2}}$ < $\sqrt{SE_1 + SE_2}$

Accordingly the study confirm that the means are significantly different that is shown by the first assumption criteria $\mu_1 - \mu_2 > 1.96\sqrt{SE_1^{\,2} + SE_2^{\,2}} = 1.25 > 0.502$
Moreover, there is no overlap between confidence interval confirms that the second condition is hold true $\mu_1 - \mu_2 > 1.96\sqrt{SE_1 + SE_2} = 1.25 > 1.19$ this result shows that there is no overlap between confidence interval.

Dixon and Massey (1983), if difference on mean of the two groups of SMEs is statistically significant then, it is always the case that the square root of the sum of squares of two numbers is less than the sum of those numbers, $\sqrt{SE_1^{\,2} + SE_2^{\,2}}$ < $\sqrt{SE_1 + SE_2}$ = $\sqrt{(.21)^2 + (.157)^2} < \sqrt{.21 + .157}$ $0.262 < 0.606$
The third condition also holds true that the square root of the sum of the square of the two groups of SMEs less than the sum of those numbers. This creates a situation where the difference in the means $(\mu_1 - \mu_2)$ increases, it becomes significantly

different before the two group mean confidence intervals cease to overlap (Hamilton, 2013).

The above two conditions hold true, implies that there is a space where the difference in the means of the two groups of SMEs is statistically significant. If the study identifies there is no confidence interval overlap, then the study can be sure that there is a significant mean difference. While the calculation for the test statistic of the difference between two means is based on the square root of the sum of squares of the standard errors. The study continues to compute a significance test on the difference between the two means of SMEs TFP with bank credit and without bank credit. For this calculation, the first step is to compute the statistic, which is simply the difference between means of the two SME groups. From the Table 6.4 above the mean of SMEs TFP with bank credit is 6.29 and the mean for the second group of SME is 5.04. The two group of SME means have different standard errors, SE_1 equal to 0.210 and SE_2 equal to 0.157 respectively. The 95 percent confidence interval for the first group mean can be calculated as: $6.29 \pm 1.96 \times 0.210$ where 1.96 is the critical t-value. The confidence interval for the first group mean is thus (3.9, 6.7). Similarly, for the second group, the confidence interval for the mean is (4.73, 5.35). Notice that the two confidence intervals overlap. However, it is erroneous to determine the statistical significance of the difference between two statistics based on overlapping confidence intervals (Hamilton, 2013). Then, further analysis has been required and then, t-statistic for comparing two means is computed as follows: $t = \frac{\mu_1 - \mu_2}{\left(\sqrt{SE_1^{\,2} + SE_2^{\,2}}\right)} = \frac{6.29 - 5.04}{\sqrt{(.21)^2 + (.157)^2}} = 4.77$ which reflects that the null hypothesis, that the mean of the two groups of SMEs are the same, should be rejected at the 0.05 confidence levels. To verify the above conclusion, consider the 95 percent confidence interval for the difference between the two group means:

$$\mu_1 - \mu_2 \pm 1.96\sqrt{SE_1^{\,2} + SE_2^{\,2}} = 1.25 \pm 1.96\sqrt{(0.21)^2 + (0.157)^2} = (0.736, 1.764)$$

Which yields (0.736, 1.764). The interval does not contain zero, hence the study reject the null hypothesis that the group means are the same. An explanation of why this is true for the case of two-sample comparison of means and the study computes the probability of getting a t value and calculates the degree of freedom.

The degrees of freedom are the number of independent estimates of variance on which standard errors is based (Fadejeva and Melihous, 2009). Accordingly, the degree of freedom can be calculated by (n_1 - 1) + (n_2 - 1), where n_1 is the sample size of bank credit recipient SMEs and n_2 is the sample size of the non-recipient SMEs. For this study, n_1 = 689 and n_2 = 853. Therefore, the degree of freedom is (688 + 852) = 1540.

Once the degree of freedom is obtained, then it is possible to calculate and find the t value of estimations of t-test on difference in mean of total factor productivity. If the confidence interval for t value does not includes 0 it right to say that there is statistically significant difference between the means of the two sample of SMEs group, at a given level of confidence (Dixon and Massey, 1983). Respectively, from the above statistical manipulation of t value estimation techniques and values the study observes that the confidence interval for the t value does not include zero.

Hence, the study has investigated that SMEs t-test on differences in mean of total factor productivity estimation model is well fitted and the study hypothesis testing result reject the null (H_0: $\mu = 0$) and support alternative hypothesis (H_1: $\mu \neq 0$). Therefore, the null hypothesis that the coefficient equals 0 would be rejected and as can be seen in Table 6.4, only t-test on difference in mean of total factor productivity is positive and statistically significant($p \leq 0.05$).

The study's null hypothesis stated that credit access has no significant effect on SMEs productivity improvement in Ethiopia while an alternative hypothesis stated that credit access improves productivity performance of Small and Medium Enterprises in Ethiopia. SMEs with bank credit have loans, revolving facilities, or both. As can be seen in Table 6.4, the coefficient estimate for the interaction term is positive and statistically significant at the 1-percent significance level (in all estimates, the reported standard errors are robust to heteroscedasticity). This result supports the hypothesis that bank credit enhances the productivity of SMEs in Ethiopia.

Then, it is factual to say that there is significant difference between the means of the two groups of SMEs, at a given level of confidence.The positive values of the t-test of the mean differences of SMEs operating with and without bank, credit implies that SME productivity is serially correlated with bank credit. The potential implication of the results is that bank credit promotes productivity and the results are more consistent with the previous findings Gatti & Love (2006), Badia & Slootmaekers (2008), Emecheta and Ibe (2014) and trade-off theory. In addition, the study finding implies that credit allows SMEs to expand or make technological improvements and investments needed to increase productivity beyond what internal funds can support.

6.5 SUMMARY OF TFP ESTIMATION RESULTS

The result implies that there is relative scarcity of capital for enterprises operating in the absence of bank credit, which are at the same time concentrated in the industry groups with numerous but small firms; capital being in short supply for small firms.

The result also shows higher returns to labour among enterprises operating with bank credit. This indicates a relative scarcity of labour in enterprises operating with bank credit, which are at the same time concentrated in the industry groups dominated by a few medium enterprises. This implies that labour is expected to be relatively scarce in medium enterprises than small enterprises. In general, enterprises with increased revenue productivity will have a higher demand for capital since each unit of capital will produce more return. An increase in the marginal cost of labour will also increase the demand for capital, which means the substitution of labour for capital will be inhabitable.

Moreover, from the TFP estimation results the study can also observed that there is a very high return to raw materials in both SMEs with and without access to bank credit. In other words, return to raw material inputs is significant in both groups of SMEs; approximately 62 percent in the credit recipient group and 60 percent in the other group, taking the average of the coefficients from the above given models (see Appendix D, table A.18).

This is further supported by enterprises' reported perception from the survey; 33 percent and 35 percent of enterprises in credit recipient and non-recipient groups 'respectively perceived shortage of raw material as a priority (see table 5.4). Possible reasons for the very high return on raw materials might be the patterns of input use and conditions of exchange rate; production function estimated using the variables capital, labour, raw materials, energy and other industrial inputs.

With regard to access to credit, which is a key variable in this study, the result from the T- test on the difference in mean value of TFP across enterprises with and without bank loan shows that there is positive relationship between SMEs productivity and access to credit in Ethiopia. A unit increase in access to credit leads to Total Factor Productivity growth of SMEs by 1.25 units. The hypothesis testing result also shows that the difference in mean value of TFP across enterprises with and without bank credit is statistically significant. Hence, the study fails to accept the null hypothesis and then support alternative hypothesis

6.6 SME PROFIT WITH ACCESS TO BANK CREDIT

This section presents the results of an empirical analysis examining SME profitability with respect to bank credit. In particular, it discusses the estimation results of equations (5) specified and illustrated in Chapter 4. These equations were presented to estimate enterprises profitability with respect to bank credit for the given years. The research looks at the extent to which bank credit has affected the profitability performance of Ethiopian manufacturing SMEs.

In line with related literature (Olutunla & Obamuyi, 2008) the profitability estimation and linear, dynamic mathematical model specified below has considered profitability as dependent variable and loans, sales, age of business, size of business and interest rate as independent variables. The model is based on firm effect performance (Mauri & Michaels, 1998; Schmalensee, 1989; Stierwald, 2010), which offers a causal theoretical explanation for firm performance in line with firm level characteristics.

Hence, the following equation stated below measures the level of SME profitability on the bases of returns on investment and key measures of performance. The regression equation is presented as follows:

$$\pi = \mu_{jt} + \gamma_1 L_{jt} + \gamma_2 Sa_{jt} + \gamma_3 A_{jt} + \gamma_4 Si_{jt} + \gamma_5 I_{jt} + \varepsilon_{jt} \ldots\ldots 5$$

Where, $\gamma_1 > 0; \gamma_2 > 0; \gamma_3 > 0; \gamma_4 > 0; \gamma_5 < 0,$

π is Profit, **Sa** is Sale, **L** is Loan, **A** is Age,

Si is size, **I** is interest, ε_{jt} and μ_{jt} are intercepts coefficient and $\gamma_1; \gamma_2; \gamma_3; \gamma_4; \gamma_5$ are parameters to be estimated.

SME profitability estimation model results presented in the table 6.6 below summarises a basic statistical figure that indicate the effects of loan dummy value on SME profitability in a given particular period of time.

Table 6.6: Bank credit and profitability of SMEs in Ethiopia, 2005-2012

Profit	Coef.	Std. Err.	t	P>|t|	[95% Conf. Interval]	
Loan dummy	-71.243	1009.079	-0.07	0.944	-2050	1908
Sales	.0000932	.0000221	4.21	0.000	.00005	.00013
Age	64.545	58.026	1.11	0.266	-49.3	178.4
Size of business	-7.073	2.897	-2.44	0.015	-12.8	-1.4
Interest rate	-1400.539	530.076	-2.64	0.008	-2440	-360
Constant	1.53e+04	5792.313	2.65	0.008	3987	2.67e+04

Source: Based on CSA survey data 2005-2012 and author's calculations

$$\pi = \mu_{jt} + -71.243\,L_{jt} + .0000932\,\mathbf{Sa}_{jt} + 64.545\,\mathbf{A}_{jt} + -7.073\,\mathbf{Si}_{jt} + -1400.539\,\mathbf{I}_{jt} + \varepsilon_{jt}$$

(0.944) (0.000) * (0.266) (0.015) * (0.008)

Note 1: *values in parenthesis are p-values and * implies significant at ten percent level*

Note 2: *Loan dummy: (Note: If an enterprise obtained a bank credit, Loan dummy=1 otherwise, Loan dummy = 0).*

Note 3: *Micro firms are excluded from these models. Firms are classified as small if the number of employees is between 10 and 19, medium if the number of employees is between 20 and 99, and large is the number of employees is above 100. Firms are classified as young when they have been operating for less than 5 years (or equal). Firms are classified as young when they have been operating for less than 10 years (or equal).*

Table 6.6 above provides the information needed to predict profitability with respect to bank credit. When the results of the study are analysed, one can observe a positive relation between indicators (total sales and age of enterprises) and profitability of the firms. The findings indicate that in Ethiopia, older firms are more profitable in comparison with young once and an increase in age of the firms causes an increase in their profitability. This may be explained by the fact that older enterprises are more effective than young enterprises since they make use of the scale economy.

This finding contradict Majumdar, (1997) arguments who discussed that in Indian younger firms are more profitable than old once. It means age variable and firms profitability have negative relationship. However, this study finds support by the previous studies (see Newman, 2010, Cole *et al.*, 2004, Vos *et al.*, 2007; Ramalho and Da Silva, 2009; Rocca *et al.*, 2009). These prior studies report that lenders find the older firms are less risky since the firms have earned a relatively good reputation over time and the lenders know most of the older firms. This situation indirectly increases the chances of utilising external financing and enhances their profitability.

On the other hand, the coefficient of credit dummy has a negative coefficient value; however, the impact on SME profitability is statistically insignificant. A one percent increase in credit dummy would result in a decrease in a profit of manufacturing SMEs by 71.24 Birr per 1000 unit. Thus, with respect to the key credit dummy variable to the SME sector, the negative relationship exhibited that an increase in bank credit to SMEs would trim down profit of Ethiopian manufacturing SMEs, but the reduction is insignificant. The results are consistent with prior studies, such as Zhao and Wijewardana (2012); Zarebski and Dimovski (2012); and Usman (2014), who found a negative association between credit impacts on the firms' profitability in support of pecking order theory. The present findings also contradict with the argument of trade-off theory that asserted firms expects a positive association between profitability and finance leverage (in this case credit access)

Thus, it can be concluded that bank credit to the SME sector has no significant effect on the profitability of Ethiopian manufacturing SMEs in a given period. The results are also consistent with the following prior studies on the area of small firms and confirm this negative relationship between firms profitability and debt financing (see Booth *et al.,* 2001; Cassar, 2001; Swinnen *et al.,* 2002; Smallbone *et al.*, 2003; Singh and Faircloth, 2005; Deakin *et al.*, 2007 and Robb and Fairlie, 2007).

On the other hand, in the regression analysis results summarised in Table 6.6 below, real bank credit amount is included in the model to find out whether it affects the profit of an enterprise. The results are consistent with both estimating profitability using credit dummy and/or actual bank credit estimates. It indicates that the amount of bank credit does not affect the enterprise profit (*p*-value =0.945>.1).

Table 6.7: Bank credit and profitability of SMEs in Ethiopia, 2006-2012

Profit	Coef.	Std. Err.	t	P>|t|	[95% Conf. Interval]
Bank credit	.0009675	.013917	0.07	0.945	-.026333 .0282681
Sales	.0932302	.0221118	4.22	0.000	.0498541 .1366064
Age	64402.24	58012.87	1.11	0.267	-49400.05 178204.5
Size of business	-7079.407	2895.508	-2.44	0.015	-12759.45 - 1399.367
Interest rate	-1397638	530359.4	-2.64	0.009	-2438029 - 357245.6
Constant	1.53e+07	5714867	2.67	0.008	4046163 2.65e+07

Source: Based on CSA survey data 2005-2012 and author's calculations

Note: *Micro firms are excluded from these models. Firms are classified as small if the number of employees is between 10 and 19, medium if the number of employees is between 20 and 99, and large is the number of employees is above*

100. Firms are classified as young when they have been operating for less than 5 years (or equal). Firms are classified as young when they have been operating for less than 10 years (or equal).

The result is not significant even at the 10 percent significant level. The overall bank credit has no significant impact on SME profitability and it does not hold for Ethiopian manufacturing SMEs.

However, it is found that *p* value of Age ($p = 0.267 < .01$) affects the output only when the time fixed -effects are not included in the model. It affects enterprise profit positively; such that, on average, one additional year of business age increases the annual profit by 64402.24 Birr holding other factors constant. Surprisingly, the size of business ($p = 0.015 < 0.01$) affects output negatively. An increase of the size of business by one permanent employee decreases the annual profit by 7079.407 Birr on average; and an increase in the interest rate ($p = 0.009 < 0.05$) by one unit decreases the annual profit by 1397638 Birr on average, holding other factors constant. The effect of *p*-value of sales ($p = 0.000 < 0.05$) on profit is to increase it as expected, and an increase in sales by one unit leads to an increase an annual profit by .0932302 Birr on average, holding other factors constant. The *p*-value of bank credit ($p = 0.945 > 0.1$) or *p*-value of access to bank credit ($p = 0.944 > 0.1$) does not affect profit.

The results of SME profitability estimation model presented in Table 6.6 show that the coefficient of real bank credit amount is positive but statistically insignificant. It shows that bank credit to the SME sector has no significant influence on manufacturing SME profitability in Ethiopia. This shows that the purpose of credit to stimulate SME profitability has not been successful. This result contradicts with prior expectations, and the study fails to accept the alternative hypothesis that assumed that bank credit is positively related to enterprise profitability.

The study result is also inconsistent with simple economic theory that suggests that access to bank credit should lead to higher profits (McMahon *et al.,* 1993). Moreover, the findings are also inconsistent with Keasey and Watson's (1991) research outcomes that argue the use of bank financing by SMEs is associated with higher profitability performance. However, the study results confirm previous studies (see Allen *et al.,* 2012, Singh and Faircloth, 2005). Such findings support the pecking order theory proposes that firms will only seek external finance when they have exhausted all sources of internal finance.

The results further implies that it is impossible to say access to credit improves SME profitability unless credit is efficiently assigned and if there are a conducive investment opportunities. Therefore, a stable and efficient supply of credit is needed in order to make profitability improvements in a context like Ethiopia. Moreover, the survey data findings indicate a clear pattern where banks lend to enterprises with lower levels of efficiency as measured by profitability and lower rates of return to capital. Conversely, banks do not lend to where efficiency and the rate of return on capital are higher. The reasons behind this need further investigation.

On the other hand, the coefficient of sales is positive and statistically significant, in conformity with prior expectations of economic theory and models of firm's profitability (Margaret, 2003). This means that profits tend to increase with an increase in sales. For profit maximising firms, a strategy to maintain a high level of profitability requires that firms must produce quality products that can easily be sold to generate more revenue, especially through effective and efficient marketing strategies. To achieve the full potential of sales, the product life cycle must be considered and the entrepreneurs must maximise the profitability during the growth stage.

Regarding business age, both old and young SMEs reported that the earliest time of the business establishment is a period of higher profits and this indicates that the business environment is not disappointing for new entrants. Furthermore, the study discovered that SME ages are positively related with profit. The argument behind this finding is that older businesses are more likely to have attained diminishing costs of production and more efficiency over some range of sales and hence are able to operate more economically and efficiently than recently established ones.

With regards to the Ethiopian business environment, the results of the positive relationship between profitability and age of business may not be unexpected. As older enterprises have greater chances to adjust them to the business environment and are involved in creative and innovative technological change. Similarly, newly established enterprises find it difficult to adjust to unfriendly business atmospheres like changing interest and exchange rates and high labour costs. Not all of which were envisaged when they started, whereas, older enterprises are more familiar with their operating area environments and therefore can more easily adjust their businesses.

Even if the coefficient of the age variable of SMEs carries a positive sign, the impacts are statistically insignificant. This implies that the age of SMEs does not have a remarkable effect on SME profitability. This result is consistent with the work of Malesky & Taussig (2009) and Allen *et al* (2012), who have found that access to bank loan does not have an effect on SMEs profitability.

The coefficient of the size of the business, measured by the number of employees, is negative and statistically significant, which is contrary to prior expectations of a positive correlation. This means that as the size of firms become bigger, less profit is expected to be realised. This is because larger firms find it difficult to cover employee's salaries and expand the business to generate a profit.

The coefficient of interest rate variable is negative and statistically significant, which confirms to a priori expectation. This implies that the profits of SMEs tend to decrease with increasing rate of interest. In Ethiopia, some SMEs have the opportunity to borrow from banks for expansion of their businesses and can enjoy the economies of scale from bulk purchasing of factors of inputs. However, the cost of credit as estimated by the level of interest rate adversely affects SMEs profitability.

In general, this study finding indicates that bank credit does not have a significant impact on SME profitability. Possible reasons might be the absence of well-established investment opportunities for SMEs in Ethiopia that may lead firms to divert credit to non-investment uses, for instance the financing of daily operations. The level of interest rate is also a cause for decline of enterprise profitability. Thus, the association of credit with SMEs profitability is all about SMEs efficiency and existing policy coordination. However, further analysis will be necessary in order to discover the reasons behind the regression results that bank credit does not have a significant impact on SMEs profitability.

6.7 ROBUSTNESS AND VALIDITY CHECK

As a robustness check, the study has estimated the production function in several different ways. For each respective SME productivity estimation model OLS estimation techniques has been applied. The first model (model-1) is a basic model where the input-output variables are directly applied to the production function. The second model (model-2) is based where material inputs and capital are lumped together. The third model (model-3) introduces a host of control variables. The study then estimate the production functions for each category separately. In all cases the study finds similar results hence, all the three SMEs productivity estimation models are robust.

Moreover, the study results remain robust to a variety of controls, alternative variables, and tests. For example, a dummy variable of access to bank credit was used to estimate SMEs profitability and later the real credit amount is included in the model with statistical results the same in the presence of multiple control variables like firm age, region, and size. Moreover, all independent variables were lagged by one year so coefficients truly reflect effects of independent variables on the output variables. In all estimations, the errors are heteroscedasticity-robust standard errors. Regressions are estimated with unweighted sample observations because the interest lies in the relationship between the independent and dependent variables. In all cases the study finds similar results hence, all the two profitability estimation models are robust and well fitted

Overall, this study results are robust to a variety of control variables, subsample choices, and productivity and profitability measures. The study results are robust to controlling for potential data related biases as well as to controlling for various SMEs characteristics. The estimation of SMEs TFP and profitability results are also robust to using alternative measures of SMEs performance.

6.8 CONCLUSIONS

This chapter has presented the main study findings from final scales purification and hypotheses testing as well as discussion of the findings. The purification was conducted through exploratory factor analysis. The study also conducted robustness tests. All measurement scales were found to possess satisfactory measurement properties. As for hypotheses testing, underlying assumptions such as outliers and multi-collinearity, were evaluated. No violation was encountered.

This chapter contributes to the external finance and enterprises performance literature by investigating to what extent the access to bank credit factors, firm-related factors, and external factors influenced the SMEs performance in terms of productivity and profitability using logistic regression tests. The chapter also presented results of multiple regression analysis that tests hypotheses. The discussion of results with the respective findings was presented accordingly in each section.

The next chapter presents a summary of the key issues that derived from this main study, contributions recommendations and limitations of the study as well as concluding the whole study by forwarding possible areas for future and further research.

CHAPTER 7: CONCLUSION AND RECOMMENDATIONS

7.1 INTRODUCTION

This study is about the understanding of relationships in the field of finance and enterprises performance. Moreover, it has important implications for the literature, SME owners and policy makers. Nonetheless, it has some limitations but also have several other possibilities for future research. This chapter presents the final remarks of the study through a summary of the findings, contributions of the study, implications of the study, limitations and suggestions for the future research. This thesis provides new features as well as reinforcing the findings of prior research.

7.2 STUDY OBJECTIVES

This section discusses the summary of the study results with respect to study objectives. The first specific objective of the study was to determine the role of access to bank credit to improve SME productivity and profitability in Ethiopia. The second objective was to test the hypothesis that bank credit enhances SMEs productivity and profitability. More specifically, this study examined whether firms with access to bank credit had relatively higher levels of performance than the other group of firms in Ethiopia. Main findings from the research can be summarised into the following categories.

7.3 REVIEW OF THE RESULTS

The purpose of the study was to fill a gap in the literature by investigating the effects of bank credit on SMEs productivity and profitability performance in Ethiopia. This section discussed the results in the context of the specific aims and objectives.

7.3.1 LEVEL OF ACCESS TO FINANCE

Evidence showed that there were credit constraints among enterprises in Ethiopia whereby SMEs were severely credit-constrained. In general, the CSA manufacturing survey data showed that SMEs in Ethiopia performed poorly across a host of finance indicators. This result confirmed that enterprises were constrained in their access to external financing sources when making investments in fixed assets such as machinery or the purchase of land. The findings are consistent with previous studies (e.g. World Bank, 2015; Dalberg, 2011; Beck *et al.,* 2008, Abdullah *et al.,* 2011) which found that small and medium enterprises are more bank credit constrained in their operation than other category of firms.

Results revealed that SMEs investment was challenged by liquidity constraints and this showed that investment decisions of manufacturing SMEs in Ethiopia were heavily dependent on cash flows. This also further implied that firms were constrained in accessing external financing sources when making investments in fixed assets such as machinery or the purchase of land.

7.3.2 BANK CREDIT AND SME PRODUCTIVITY

To emphasise the importance of access to bank credit practices on SME productivity, the hypothesis of a difference in mean of TFP of two groups of SMEs was tested. Results revealed that the mean of TFP value for SMEs that were operating with access to bank credit was slightly higher than that of SMEs that were "not efficient" in credit accessing practices. The study hypothesis testing result also showed that the difference in mean value of TFP across the two groups of SMEs was statistically significant. Hence, the study failed to accept the null hypothesis. In this regard, the study had recognized the stated alternative hypothesis that access to credit had an observed effect on SMEs total factor productivity in Ethiopia. The results are consistent with prior studies, such as Butler & Cornaggia (2007), Lashitew (2011), Badia & Slootmaekers (2008), Gatti & Love (2006), Emecheta and Ibe (2014), who asserted that finance access is a key determining factor to enhance enterprise performance in terms of boosting productivity.

7.3.3 BANK CREDIT AND SME PROFITABILITY

The study also further explored the effects of bank credit access on SME profitability and the results showed that there was no interdependence between SME profitability and bank credit. In other words, there is no statistically significant relationship between profit of manufacturing SMEs in Ethiopia and bank credit. The results support pecking-order theory that firms prefer internal funds in financing decisions and by that strategy will have less external funds such as debt or external equity. However, these results contradicted empirical studies by Olutunla & Obamuyi (2008) and Shinozaki (2012). These prior studies reported that access to bank credit has a significant positive impact on SMEs profitability performance.

In addition, results indicate that only sales, business size and interest rate have a significant association with SME's profitability performance. Results also revealed that bank credit and SMEs age have insignificant effect with SME's profitability. The results are consistent with prior studies, such as Malesky & Taussig (2009) and Allen *et al* (2012) who found that access to bank credit does not have an effect on enterprises profitability. Such findings support the pecking order theory that proposes that firms will only seek external finance when they have exhausted all sources of internal finance and contradicts trade-off and cash flow theories.

7.4 CONCLUSION OF THE FINDINGS

The view that credit promotes SME productivity and profitability is a shared idea and it aligns with trade-off and cash flow theories. Credit allows many productive SMEs to grow or make technological improvements and investments needed to increase productivity beyond what their internal funds can support at all stages of a business. Under these conditions, credit is efficiently assigned if there is soft credit interest rate policy, and suitable and supportive business environment.

The study tries to understand whether SMEs with access to bank credit have relatively higher levels of productivity and profitability or the other way round. To address this objective the study used fixed effect regression model and neoclassical economic theory to specify the relationship between access to credit and SMEs productivity. Moreover, the study used linear, dynamic mathematical model to estimate the effects of bank credit on SMEs profitability. The study also applied inferential statistical techniques such as OLS (ordinary least square) for measuring the significance level, and multivariate analysis to test the hypothesis of association.

The following main conclusions can be drawn from the study: First, the study proves that SMEs that are run by individuals who have access to bank credit have slightly higher level of total factor productivity (TFP). More precisely, the study found that average TFP among enterprises with access to bank credit is 1.25 times higher than enterprises with no access to a bank credit. Hypothesis testing result also revealed that the difference in mean value of TFP across enterprises with and without bank credit is positive, statistically significant and confirms that bank credit improves SME's productivity. The findings are consistent with previous studies done by Gatti and Love (2006), Butler and Cornaggia (2007), Lashitew (2011), Emecheta and Ibe (2014).

Second, the study explored the effects of bank credit access on SME profitability and showed that there was no interdependence between SME profitability and bank credit. In other words, there was no statistically significant relationship between a profit of manufacturing SMEs and bank credit in Ethiopia. Hence, the positive impact of bank credit on SME profitability observed in other studies (for example Olutunla & Obamuyi, 2008; Shinozaki, 2012) do not apply in the Ethiopian context. Instead, firms that rely on alternative and internal sources of finance alone were not less performing than those with access to bank credit were. The study confirmed the results of previous studies (Malesky & Taussig, 2009 and Allen *et al.*, 2012). Such findings support the pecking order theory that proposes, firms will only seek external finance when they have exhausted all sources of internal finance and contradicts trade-off and cash flow theories.

Insignificant and negative relationship between credit and SMEs' profitability revealed that the Ethiopian manufacturing SMEs did not use credit as a control mechanism to maximise the profitability performance as stated by agency theory. It is not possible to recommend high credit levels to SMEs owner-managers within the study sample because of the negative relationship between credit and profitability performance. It explains that borrowing hastened the separation between SMEs and lenders. The result indicated that like most of the firms in the world (Phillips and Sipahioglu, 2004); SMEs in Ethiopia are attempting to grow through less risky paths and this idea aligns with pecking order theory. In addition, results indicated that only sales and size of the business have a positive and statistically significant association with SMEs profitability performance while bank credit and SMEs age have a positive but statistically insignificant association with SMEs profitability performance.

The results further implied that the current emphasis by the government to enhance credit access as a strategy for improving profitability performance within the manufacturing SMEs sector may not yield the desired results unless other simultaneous efforts and steps undertaken. Credit access by itself without suitable investment opportunity may also lead

SMEs' to divert credit to non-investment uses, for instance, the financing of daily operations. Another potential reason could be the amount of interest rate (high cost of loans) and bank loan volumes may be too small for making a significant impact on SME profitability. That might have an adverse impact on SME profitability. Thus, the channel of transmission from credit to productivity and profitability matters. Moreover, in developing countries in general and in Ethiopia in particular, bank lending is based too much on political connections so credit may not go to profitable SMEs, or the level and amount of credit may matter for the firms to be efficient and profitable.

7.5 CONTRIBITION OF THE STUDY

This study was based on financial management, economic growth and small business to develop a theoretical framework to explain the effects of external finance on SMEs performance in Ethiopia. A variety of economic theories were explored from neoclassical economic theory (Tinbergen, 1942), pecking order theory (Myers, 1984; Myers and Majluf, 1984), life-cycle model (Modigliani and Brumberg, 1954), static trade-off theory (DeAngelo and Masulis, 1980), , agency theory (Jensen and Meckling, 1976) and Solow (1957) productivity model. The concern of these theories aids in resolving inconsistent results concerning the influence of bank credit access on SMEs' productivity and profitability. Consequently, this study contributed to the existing body of knowledge.

This study has contributed to existing literature by providing further evidence on the link between access to credit and firm performance using productivity and profitability as the measure of performance indicators. The study also provided empirical evidence on link between source of credit and firm productivity.

Studying the influence of access to bank credit on SMEs performance on developing countries context will be more worthy especially in the wake of the current economic dynamics as suggested by Deesomsak *et al.* (2004). In essence, this thesis attempted to bring the description of developed world financial theory together with actual financing practices of firms from other economic backgrounds, thus bridge the gap between theory and practice.

Previous studies in developing countries have focused on factors affecting access to credit by SMEs (Kimuyu and Omiti, 2000; Green *et al.*, 2002; Atieno, 2009). Less attention has been given to establish whether access to credit improves the performance of SMEs. According to Nkurunziza (2010), use of credit may have a positive impact on firm's performance if it helps the firm to address its liquidity constraints, or it can have a negative impact when there are shocks in the economy leading to increased interest rates.

This is the first empirical study to examine the dual effects of access to bank credit on SMEs' productivity and profitability in Ethiopia from manufacturing industry perspectives. Although the government is providing better financial and technical support to assist SMEs, the effects of these policies have not been subject to systematic analysis until now. This study provides evidence that there is a significant (partially) mediating role of access to bank credit on the firm's productivity performance. On the other hand, the same study provides evidence that there is negative and statistically insignificant relation between access to bank credit and SMEs profitability.

7.5.1 THEORETICAL FRAMEWORK

The model developed in this thesis was a simple model, adapted from various models (see Osei-Assibey, 2013; Wolf, 2007; Solow, 1957; Tinbergen, 1942; Ferri, 1981; Baily et al, 1992). In terms of theory, predominantly classical economic theory, trade-off theory, pecking-order theory, cash-flow theory, firm-productivity growth theory and framework have been considered to develop respective SMEs productivity and profitability estimation models.

The assumption behind in developing and using these models was positive relationships between access to bank credit and SME productivity and profitability. This was because; the notion that credit promotes firm's performance is shared knowledge among entrepreneurs' policy makers and owners. Credit allows many business enterprises to expand or make technological advancements and investments needed to increase their profit beyond what their internal funds can allow.

However, the findings are mixed and went in a different direction. This could help to consider certain issues with respect to access to bank credit to SMEs, like the level of credit efficiency, interest rate regulations and environment for investment opportunities to allocate the loan to the most solid, profitable and productive businesses. Overall, the proposed firm's productivity growth theory, profit maximisation behaviour and framework can help in understanding and formulating appropriate response strategies in line with investment opportunities and the level of interest rate regulation.

7.5.2 CONTRIBUTION TO THE LITRATURES

By balancing prior research outcomes and present study's contributions, the thesis contributes to the body of knowledge and presents some implications for policy makers to practice. For academics, this study adds to the streams of research that explains the importance of the decision to use bank credit to improve SMEs performance. The study takes different perspective, by providing evidences from access to bank credit, namely considering the influence of bank credit on SMEs performance.

In summary, the SMEs ability to improve its productivity or profitability constitutes an essential drive to face financing constraints challenges, and associated with bank bureaucratic procedure.

This study is one of the few that are actually based on empirical data from developing country's contexts and it helps to gain better understanding of SMEs financing, productivity and profitability in Ethiopia. The thesis adds to the financial studies literature by developing an integrated model that combines two perspectives; on the access to bank credit, SMEs productivity and SMEs profitability. From the existing literature, there was an unclear and inconclusive view on what effect access to bank credit has on the sensitivities of SMEs' performance.

This study proposed an explanation that reconciles the conflicting empirical evidence on the study topic. The study has presented two models; the *productivity model*, in which SMEs use bank credit to improve productivity, and the *profitability model*, in which SMEs' use bank credit to improve profitability. However, most of the previous literatures focused mainly on firms' profitability or productivity rather than using both performance indicators simultaneously.

This study analysed the dual effects of bank credit on SME profitability and productivity and its findings contributed to the often contradictory or inconclusive literature on finance, firm productivity and profitability using different statistical methods at firm level. The research on the topic of finance and SME performance is much more limited and there is a debate about whether bank credit exerts any effects on firm's total factor productivity and profitability.

The novelty of this empirical analysis was twofold: (i) it considered both productivity and profitability performance indicators and identified the effects of bank credit access on SMEs performance measures for specific types of enterprises, industries and developing countries at a given period of time. (ii) It used a unified econometric framework and analysed the effects of bank credit on SMEs productivity and profitability over and above demand and cyclical factors across manufacturing SMEs. Therefore, the study contributes to the often contradictory or inconclusive debate on the topic. Hence, this study makes a methodological contribution to the literature by using methodological triangulation to investigate the effects of bank credit on SMEs productivity and profitability performance.

This thesis also contributed to the literature on access to external finance and SMEs performance. Furthermore, the present thesis has focused on bank credit as one important dimension of factors of inputs and its impact on SMEs productivity and profitability. To better, comprehend the effect of access to bank credit on SMEs performance. The study emphasised several areas where such an understanding can complement and extend traditional strategy and frameworks and perspectives.

Finally, the study adds empirical evidence to the stream of research that explains the antecedents of the decision to bank credit access. In this sense, the study argued that access to finance leads to improve SMEs productivity. However, the impact is insignificant on SMEs profitability in Ethiopia. The study can state that, while most of studies (Olutunla & Obamuyi, 2008; Shandker, 2012; Khandker *el at,* 2013; Allen *el at;* 2012; Gatti & Love, 2006; Badia and Slootmaekers, 2008; Butler and Cornaggia, 2007; Lashitew, 2011) analysed a single effects of bank credit by taking either SMEs profitability or productivity as dependent variable not both performance indicators at the same time. So, in relative terms, this study gave a more comprehensive reflection of SMEs performance in developing countries.

7.5.3 CONTRIBUTION TO SME OWNERS

From a practical perspective, this thesis provides meaningful lessons for SME owners and managers. First, the study argues that it is important or crucial to know the effectiveness of bank credit usage as financial resource in order to achieve maximum benefits out of it. That is, SME owners and managers should recognize the significance of borrowing from bank related to ties to secure necessary factor inputs that might promote productivity efficiency and have an impact on SMEs performance.

Finally, this thesis have also showed that access to bank credit allow SMEs more likely to operate beyond their border. That is on the one hand, the study finding emphasize that access to bank credit has a significant impact on the SMEs productivity. On the other hand, the study findings revealed that access to bank credit does not have any bottom line impact to improve SMEs profitability. Thus, SMEs owners and managers should choose whether to engage in borrowing from bank or not by applying cost benefit analysis.

Finally, this study identifies the critical factors that might accelerate the performance of SMEs. This study will give benefit to SME owners-managers in aiding them to choose the right financing capital for their firms. Findings of the relevance of finance related theories in explaining firms' financing behaviours suggest that both pecking order and agency coexist in Ethiopia. Current findings suggest that SMEs owner-managers should concentrate on internally generated funds in order to gain the most from profitability perspective. However, sometimes owner-managers may overlook the opportunities to enhance the value if they do not utilise debt. Thus, owner-managers may acquire external funds with the condition that they should fit decisions around taking full advantage out of using bank credit financing.

7.6 RECOMENDATIONS

7.6.1 RESEARCH AND DEVELOPMENT

Financing SMEs is a relatively popular research area, and current international level research is developing innovative ideas in this area. Hence, there is a need to promote the production of such knowledge towards the dynamic nature of the issue by strengthening linkages and knowledge exchanges between researchers, financing institutions, entrepreneurs, investors and practitioners. Moreover, it is useful to provide stakeholders with all information that is essential in the intervention and adaptation process of SME financing, especially in developing countries.

Previous studies in developing countries have focused on factors affecting access to credit by SMEs (Kimuyu and Omiti, 2000; Green *et al.*, 2002; Atieno, 2009). Less attention has been paid to establish whether access to credit improves the performance of SMEs. According to Nkurunziza (2010), use of credit can have a positive impact on firm's performance if it helps the firm to address its liquidity constraints, or it can have a negative impact, when there are shocks in the economy leading to increased interest rates.

Moreover, the study findings are important additions to the ongoing exercise of understanding what makes SMEs productive and profitable in the market if external source of funds are available. It should be treated as a basis for future studies on understanding SMEs financing dynamics and productivity and profitability in a broader sense.

7.6.2 BANKING SECTOR

Implications of the study can also be drawn for financial institutions engaging in lending to SMEs. Many SMEs are averse to borrow from financial institutions due to strict lending requirements. Financial institutions should consider changing their credit policies accordingly to suit the individual conditions of the firm, and not solely assess the creditworthiness of the firm based on past performance. Financial institutions might consider placing greater weight on other factors such as the viability of its future business plans or growth potential of the firm. They might also consider accepting more items as collateral (i.e. other than fixed assets such as receivables, inventory and equipment) as suggested by Fagan and Zhao (2009).

The study also recommended that the National Bank of Ethiopia should take the lead to create a platform for knowledge sharing and exposure for best practices in SMEs financing in Ethiopia. This may help to have a common consensus on SMEs financing among stockholders, and targeting the Ethiopian Banker's Association and MFI would be a good approach to take.

7.6.3 PUBLIC SECTOR

The importance of SMEs for the development of the Ethiopian economy is undeniable. Current research also confirms that access to finance for SMEs significantly improve productivity. Hence, there is a need to ensure that policies in various sectors (Finance, SME development and industrialisation) are integrated to enhance the role of SMEs in Ethiopia.

In order to effectively address the SMEs financing problems, the government of Ethiopia should consider and adopt an integrated approach towards creating SMEs financing culture among financial institutions. A stable and efficient supply of credit is needed in order to make SMEs productivity improvements, particularly in Ethiopia. In addition to this, the government of Ethiopia should encourage financial institutions to improve the financing environment for SMEs, strengthen support to SMEs in terms of enhanced credit facilities with possible minimum interest rate.

Research on the optimal structure of interventions would help to increase the financial and social sustainability of SME and increased research and empirical evidence will help to further strengthen the case to support SMEs and the effectiveness of specific interventions. SME productivity analysis with respect to finance access allows gaining picture of SME financing in Ethiopia. In general, additional research on the overall impact of capital provision to different types of SMEs would be helpful for the overall advocacy for SME interventions. Furthermore, one of the serious challenges for SMEs is limited access to finance to purchase inputs necessary to adjust their business systems to suit a changing market. In this regard, the government and other developmental agencies should intervene, for example, through the provision of subsidies, to ensure that enterprises have access to such inputs.

Moreover, the findings indicated that access to bank credit and SMEs productivity performance could be valuable to a society as a whole. It represents more than just finance topics and have direct influence on potentially successful SMEs. Particularly in the Ethiopian context the study, make it easier for public support agencies to identify SMEs with resource and potential growth.

The important contribution of this study was; the knowledge and understanding of effects of providing credit access on SMEs performance are prerequisites in the adaptation process. One important aspect is to bring out the key issues that need attention when promoting SMEs financing and adaptation at the policy level. An important contribution to practice is that there is a need to embrace all the policy initiatives and channels to support SMEs.

7.7 LIMITATIONS

Similar to other empirical research conducted in the field of finance and firm's performance; the conclusions drawn in this thesis are based on organisational behaviours at a particular time. Thus, any development beyond August 2012 is unaccounted because the study used CSA data of Ethiopia for the period of 2005-2012.

The satisfactory results of tests for generalisability and non-response bias allowed the findings to be generalised only to SMEs within World Bank SMEs definition criteria provided in Tables 2.3 in this study. Hence, it would be misleading and inappropriate to make a claim that the findings of this research were applicable across all SMEs in Ethiopia. It is to be noted here that, this study was limited to SMEs in manufacturing sector. Owing to the above limitations, this study cannot be generalized including all the SMEs in Ethiopia.

The results are representative of SMEs in Ethiopia and are not necessarily generalizable to other countries. It is important to be aware of the cultural, legal, and institutional differences between developing and developed economies as highlighted by

Chen (2004). The findings of this study may be limited to the Ethiopian context and may not be necessarily reflecting access to bank credit and SMEs performance behaviours in other countries. However, the limitations and generalisability issues do not minimise the significance of the findings. Alternatively, these limitations provide scope for other studies to further test and extend the theoretical framework developed in this thesis.

7.8 AREAS FOR FURTHER RESEARCH

This study also suggests important areas for further research. The further research question may arise, why the fact of receiving a bank credit in and of itself is not to be good for profitability in Ethiopian manufacturing SMEs sector. By taking additional controlling variables like the amount spent in loan repayment and the duration of repayment, threshold of the loan amount and the existing investment opportunities into consideration the study can be further enriched. Extending the study in this way would enrich the policy recommendations of the government for enhancing the performance of the SMEs sector.

Another potential research area could be related with CSA of Ethiopia survey data and the data is collected in an annual basis. It is an excellent resource to do a follow up and extension of the research with the next available survey data (coverage 2013-2016) and it would make possible to see the sustainability of the impacts of bank credit on SMEs performance over time. As a follow up, this could relatively be the next research agenda.

The theoretical framework developed in this study can be used as the basis for future research into the financing of SMEs in other developing countries. Future research is needed to compare the financing behaviours of SMEs in Ethiopia with those in other developing countries. Further investigations may lead to explore the differences in industries and sectors to enhance the knowledge of SMEs' financing needs. In addition, it would be useful to conduct a comparative study of company and non-company financing behaviours as these two structures have their own special characteristics arising from their legal status and the extent of limited liability and financial disclosure.

The empirical works for this research were undertaken in Ethiopia. The selection (Ethiopia as a research context) followed the suggestion of Thong (1999) who stated that there are many differences between developing countries like Ethiopia and developed countries. Hence, it would be interesting to compare the findings of one part of the world to those of other parts.

REFERENCES

Abdullah, M. A., Manan, S. K. A., and Khadijah, S. (2011). Small and Medium Enterprises and Their Financing Patterns: Evidence from Malaysia. *Journal of Economic Cooperation and Development*, 32(2), *p.* 1-18.

Abebe, A. (2012) 'Rule by law in Ethiopia: Rendering Constitutional Limits on Government Power Nonsensical', CGHR Working Paper 1, Cambridge: University of Cambridge Centre of Governance and Human Rights

Abegaz, T. M. (2013). Total Factor Productivity and Technical Efficiency in the Ethiopian Manufacturing Sector. *Ethiopian Development Institute.* Department of Economics, Addis Ababa University, EDRI Working Paper 10.

Abor, J., and Biekpe, N. (2009). How Do We Explain the Capital Structure of SMEs in Sub-Saharan Africa? Evidence from Ghana. *Journal of Economic Studies*, 36(1), *p.* 83-97.

Abor, J., and Biekpe, N. (2007). Small business reliance on bank financing in Ghana. *Emerging Markets Finance and Trade,* 43(4), *p.* 93-102.

Addison and Geda. (2001), Ethiopia's New Financial Sector and its Regulation, *World Institute for Development Economics Research,* Discussions Paper No. 2001/55

Adèr, H. J., and Mellenbergh, G. J. (1999). Research Methodology in the Social Behavioural and Life Sciences. SAGE (online).

African Development Bank Group (ADBG, 2011). Federal Democratic Republic of Ethiopia Country Strategic Paper (2011-2015)

Ageba, G., and Amha, W. (2004), *Micro and Small Enterprises Development in Ethiopia: Survey Report, January 2004),* Ethiopian Development Research Institute (EDRI) (2004)

Ahn, S. (2000). "Firm Dynamics and Productivity Growth: A Review of Micro Evidence from OECD Countries", OECD Economics Department Working Paper No. 297

Al-Ajmi, J., Hussain, H. A., and Al-Saleh, N. (2009). Decisions on capital structure in a 'Zakat' environment with prohibition of 'riba': The case of Saudi Arabia. *The Journal of Risk Finance, 10*(5), *p.* 460-476.

Alexander, W., and Cornaggia, J. B. (2007). Does Access to Finance Improve Productivity? Evidence from a Natural Experiment *World Bank Policy Research.* University of Texas World Bank.

Alfaro, A., Kalemli-Ozcan, S., and Sayek, S. (2009). FDI, Productivity and Financial Development. *The world Economy Journal compilation* © Blackwell Publishing Ltd.

Allayannis, George, and Abon Mozumdar, 2001, The investment-cash flow sensitivity puzzle: Can negative cash flow observations explain it? Working paper, University of Virginia.

Allen, F., and Oura, H. (2004). Sustained Economic Growth and the Financial System. IMES Discussion Paper Series 2004-E-17 August 2004

Allen, F., Chakrabarti, R., De, S., Qian, J. Q., and Qian, M. (2012). Financing Firms in India. *Journal of Financial Intermediation*, 21(3), *p.* 409-445.

Alti, Aydogan, 2003, How sensitive is investment to cash flow when financing is frictionless? *Journal of Finance* 58, *p.* 707-722.

Altenburg, T. (2010). Industrial Policy in Ethiopia. Discussion Paper 2/2010. German Development Institute

Andrea, A. (2009). Introduction to Econometrics. University of Bologna and Cepr. Course works outline series

Ang and McKibbini. (2006). Financial Liberalization, Financial Sector Development and Growth; Evidence from Malaysia, *Journal of Economic Development* 84(2007), *p.* 215-233

Angelo, B. G., Tamagni, F. S., and Anna, S. S. (2007). Productivity, Profitability and Financial Fragility: Empirical Evidence from Italian Business Firms. *Laboratory of Economics and Management*, Working paper series.

Asiedu, E., Kalonda-Kanyama, I., Ndikumana, L., and Nti-Addae, A. (2013). "Access to Credit by Firms in Sub-Saharan Africa: How Relevant is Gender?" PERI Working Paper

Atkinson, D. R. (2013). Competitiveness, Innovation and Productivity: Clearing up the Confusion. The *Information Technology & Innovation Foundation*

Arestis, P., Demetriades, P., and Fattouh, B. (2003). "Financial Policies and the Aggregate Productivity of the Capital Stock: Evidence from Developed and Developing Economies," *Eastern Economic Journal*, Vol. 29, No. 2, Spring.

Ashenafi, B. (2012). Banking Reform and SMME Financing in Ethiopia: Evidence from Manufacturing Sector. *African Journal of Business Management, Academic journal, 6(19)*

Assefa, B., Zerfu, A., and Tekle, B. (2014). Identifying Success Factors and Constraints in Ethiopia's MSE Development: An Explanatory Research. Ethiopian Development Research Institute Addis Ababa, Ethiopia October 2014

Atieno, R., (2009). "Linkages, Access to Finance and the Performance of Small-Scale Enterprises in Kenya." Research Paper No. 2009/06, *World Institute for Development Economic Research,* United Nation University, Nairobi.

Ayed., W. H. B., and Zouari, S. G. (2014). Capital structure and financing of SMEs: The Tunisian case. *International Journal of Economics and Finance*, 6(5), *p.* 96.

Banham, H., and He, Y. (2009), 'SME Governance: Converging Definitions and Expanding Expectations'. Presentation to the 9th Annual Clute International Business and Economic Research Conference, Las Vegas, October 2009.

Babajid, A. (2012). Effects of Microfinance on Micro and Small Enterprises (SMEs) Growth in Nigeria. *Asian Economic and Finance Review*, 2(3): *p.* 463-477.

Badia, M. M. & Slootmaekers, V. (2008): The Missing Link between Financial Constraints and Productivity

Bailey, K. D. (1994). Methods of Social Research. *The Free Press*, New York.

Baily, M. N., Hulten, C., and Campbell, D. (1992). "Productivity Dynamic in Manufacturing Plants" Brooking Papers on Economic Activity: Microeconomic, *p.* 187-267

Baker, M., and Wurgler, J. (2002). Market Timing and Capital Ctructure. *The Journal of Finance,* 57, *p.* 1-30.

Balcha, L. L., Serbeh-Yiadom K. C., and Asfaw, M. (2014). The Role of Ethiopian Medium and Large Scale Manufacturing Industries in Strengthening Rural-Urban Linkages. Developing Country Studies www.iiste.org ISSN 2224-607X, Vol.4, No.9, 2014.

Baltensperger, E., and Devinney, M. T. (1985). Credit Rationing Theory: A Survey and Synthesis. *Journal of Institutional and Theoretical Economics*, Bd. 141, H. 4, *p.* 475-502. http://www.jstor.org/stable/40750797. Accessed: 30-03-2016 11:53 UTC

Bancel, F., and Mittoo, U. R. (2004). Cross-Country Determinants of Capital Structure Choice: A survey of European firms. *Financial Management.* 33(4), *p.* 103-132.

Bany-Ariffin, A. N., Mat Nor, F., and McGowan Jr, C. B. (2010). Pyramidal Structure, Firm Capital Structure Exploitation and Ultimate Owners' Dominance. *International Review of Financial Analysis*, 19(3), *p.* 151-164.

Barros, L. A., Nakamura, W. T., and Forte, D. (2013). Determinants of the capital structure of small and medium sized Brazilian enterprises. *BAR-Brazilian Administration Review*, 10(3), *p.* 347-369.

Bartelsman, E., and Mark, D. (2000). "Understanding Productivity: Lessons from Longitudinal Microdata", Journal of Economic Literature, Vol. 38, No. 3, September, *p.* 569-594.

Batu, M. M. (2016). Drivers of Ethiopian Economic Growth: A Systematic Review. *International Journal of Science.* Volume 6, Issue 3, ISSN 2250-3153

Basu, S., Kimball, and Miles S. (1997). Cyclical Productivity with Unobserved Input Variation. NBER Working Paper, No. 5915, February 1997.

Baxter, L. A., and Babbie, E. (2004). The Basic of Communication Research. Belmont, CA: Wadsworth.

Beattie, V., Goodarce, A., and Thomson, S. J. (2006). Corporate Financing Decisions: UK survey evidence. *Journal of Business, Finance and Accounting*, 33(9/10), *p.* 1402 -1434.

Beck, T., and Cull, R. (2014). Small and Medium Sized Enterprises Finance in Africa. African Growth Institute Working Paper 16/ July 2014.

Beck, L., and Laoayz. (1999). Finance and Sources of Growth. *Journal of Economics,* 58(2): *p.* 261-300

Beck, S. M. (1974). Determining the Importance of an Independent Variable: A Path Analytic Solution *Social Science Research*, 3, 95-107 (1974) Lewis- University of Michigan, Ann Arbor, Michigan

Beck, T., Levine, R., and Loayza, N. (2000), "Financial Intermediation and Growth: Causality and Causes," *Journal of Monetary Economics*, Vol. 46, p. 31-77.

Beck, T., Demirgüç-Kunt, A., and Maksimovic, V. (2008). Financing Patterns Around the World: Are small firms different?. *Journal of Financial Economics*, 89(3), *p.* 467-487.

Beck, T., Demirguc-Kunt, A., and Peria, S. M. (2008). "Bank Financing for SMEs around the World: Drivers, Obstacles, Business Models, and Lending Practices." *World Bank Policy Research Working Report* 4785. Washington, DC

Beck , T., A. Demirgüç-Kunt, and M. S. M. Peria. (2007). "Reaching out: Access to and Use of Banking Services across Countries." Journal of Financial Economics 85: *p.* 234-66.

Beck, T., and Demirguc-Kunt, A. (2006). Small and medium-size enterprises: Access to finance as a growth constraint. Journal of Banking & Finance, 30(11), *p.* 2931-2943.

Beck, T., Demirguc-Kunt, A., and Maksimovic, V. (2005). "Financial and Legal Constraints to Growth: Does Firm Size Matter?" *Journal of Finance* 60 (1):137–177.

Beck, L. and Laoayz, N. (1999). Finance and Sources of Growth. *Journal of Economics,* 58(2): *p.* 261-300

Bekele, E. and Worku, Z. (2008). Factors that Affect the Long Term Survival of Micro, Small and Medium Enterprises in Ethiopia. *South African Journal of Economics*, 76(3): *p.* 548-568

Berg, G., Fuchs, M., L. Iacovone, T. Jaeggi, A. Lovegrove, and C. Villegas Sanchez. 2012. Financing Small and Medium Enterprises in the Nigeria. World Bank. Washington, DC.

Berger, A. N., and Udell, G. F. (1998). The Economics of Small Business Finance: The Roles of Private Equity and Debt Markets in the Financial Growth Cycle. *Journal of Banking and Finance,* 22(6-8), *p.* 613-673.

Bevan, A. A., and Danbolt, J. (2002). Capital Structure and its Determinants in the UK: A Decomposition analysis. *Applied Financial Economics*, 12(3), *p*.159-170.

Bezabeh, A., and Desta, A. (2014) "Banking Sector Reform in Ethiopia". *Collected Faculty Scholarship*. Paper 96. http://scholar.dominican.edu/all-faculty/96

Bhaduri, S. (2002). Determinants of Corporate Borrowing: Some evidence from the Indian corporate structure. *Journal of Economics and Finance*. 26(2), Summer, *p*. 200-215.

Biesebroeck, V. J. (2008). "The Sensitivity of Productivity Estimates: Revisiting Three Important Debates." *Journal of Business and Economic Statistics*, 26(3): *p*. 311-28.

Biesebroeck, V. J. (2005). "Exporting Raises Productivity in Sub-Saharan African Manufacturing Firms." *Journal of International Economics*, 67(2): *p*. 373-91.

Biewen, M., and Weiser, C. (2011) A New Approach to Testing Marginal Productivity Theory. Discussion Paper No. 6113 November 2011

Bigsten, A., and Gebreeyesus, M. (2009). Productivity and Exports: Evidence from Ethiopian manufacturing, in: *Journal of Development Studies*, 45 (10), *p*. 1594-1614

Bigsten, A. and Gebreeyesus, M. (2007). The Small, the Young, and the Productive: Determinants of Manufacturing Firm Growth in Ethiopia. *Chicago Journal Economic Development and Cultural Change*, Vol. 55, No. 4 (July 2007), p. 813-840. http://www.jstor.org/stable/10.1086/516767

Birara, A. (2010). Waves Endemic Poverty that Globalization can't Tackle but Ethiopians can. www.sbpbooks.com

Black, R. R. (1999). Doing Qualitative Research in the Social Sciences. London: SAGE

Black, S. E., and Strahan, P. E. (2002). Entrepreneurship and Bank Credit Availability. *Journal of Finance* 57: *p*. 2807-2833.

Bloom, N., Mahajan, A., McKenzie, D., and Roberts, J. (2010). Why Do Firms in Developing Countries Have Low Productivity? *American Economic Review*: Papers & Proceedings 2010, 100:2, *p.* 619–623

Boland, P. J. (2000). William Sealy Gosset-alias 'Student' 1876-1937. *In Creators of Mathematics*: The Irish Connection, ed. K. Houston, 105–112. Dublin: University College Dublin Press.

Booth, L., Aivazian, V., Demirguc-Kunt, A., and Maksimovic, V. (2001). Capital Structure in Developing Countries. *Journal of Finance,* 56(1), *p.* 87-130.

Borgia, D., and Newman, A. (2012). The Influence of Managerial Factors on the Capital Structure of Small and Medium-sized Enterprises in Emerging Economies: Evidence from China. *Journal of Chinese Entrepreneurship*, 4(3), *p.* 180-205.

Bottazzi, G., Secchi, A., and Tamagni, F. (2006). "Financial Fragility and Growth Dynamics of Italian Business Firms", LEM Working Papers 2006/7, Sant'Anna School of Advanced Studies, Pisa, Italy

Bouri, A., Breij, M., Diop, M., Kempner, R., Klinger, B., and Stevenson, K. (2011). Report on Support to SMEs in Developing Countries through Financial Intermediaries

Boyer, D., Creech, H., and Paas, L. (2008). Critical Success Factors and Performance Measures for Start-up Social and Environmental Enterprises. Supporting Entrepreneurs for Sustainable Development. Report for SEED Initiative Research Programme:

Brewer, J., and Hunter, A. (2006). Foundations of Multi Method Research: synthesizing styles. SAGE, Thousand Oaks, California.

Brigham, E., and Ehrhardt, M. (2013). *Financial management: Theory and practice*. Cengage Learning.

Brixiova, Z. (2009). On Determinants of SME start-ups in Ethiopia: A Theoretical Exploration; African

Development Bank, Development Research Department, Tunis, Tunisia

Burk and Rhoads. (1985). Profits and Contestability*:* State by State Evidence from *Banking Markets Review of Industrial Organization volume* 4 No. 2, *p.* 59-77

Burns, P. (1985). Financial Characteristics of Small Companies in the UK, Cranfield School of Management

Butler, W. A., and Cornaggia, J. (2007). Does Access to Finance Improve Productivity? Evidence from a Natural Experiment. *World Bank Policy Research.* University of Texas World Bank.

Cameron, A. C. and Trivedi, K. P. (2005). Micro Econometrics. Methods and Applications, *Cambridge University Press, U.K.*

Carlin, W., and Mayer, C. (2003). "Finance, Investment and Growth." *Journal of Financial Economics* 69, *p.* 191-226.

Carpenter, R. E., and Petersen, B. C. (2002). Capital Market Imperfections, High-Tech Investment, and New Equity Financing. *The Economic Journal*, 112(477), *p.* F54-F72.

Carpnter, R. E., and Bruce C. P. (2002)."Is the Growth of Small Firms Constrained by Internal Finance?, *The Review of Economics and Statistics*, MIT Press, vol. 84(2), pages 298-309, May.

Cassar, G. (2004). The Financing of Business Start-ups. *Journal of Business Venturing,* 19(2), *p.* 261-283.

Cassar, G., and Holmes, S. (2003). Capital Structure and Financing of SMEs: Australian Evidence. *Accounting and Finance*, 43(2), *p.* 123-147.

Cavallo. E., Arizala. F., and Galindo, A. (2009). Financial Development and TFP Growth: Cross-Country and Industry-Level Evidence. Inter-American Development *Bank Working Paper #682 RG-K1097*

Cecchetti, S. G., and Kharroubi, E. (2012). Reassessing the Impact of Finance on Growth (No.381). *Bank for International Settlements*

Central Statistics Agency (CSA, 2004). Report on Bio-annual Employment, Unemployment Survey, 1st year Round two Statistical Bulletins, Addis Ababa.

Central Statistical Agency (CSA, 2011). Report on Large and Medium Scale Manufacturing and Electricity Industries Survey Addis Ababa, August 2011. http://www.csa.gov.et/newcsaweb/images/documents/surveys/Industries_Survey/Industries_Survey_2009/survey0/data/Doc/Reports/LMMIS_2009-2010%20Report.pdf

Central Statistical Agency (CSA, 2014). Ethiopia Mini Demographic and Health Survey

Central Statistical Agency (CSA, 2011). Report on Large and Medium Scale Manufacturing and Electricity Industries Survey Addis Ababa, August 2011. http://www.csa.gov.et/newcsaweb/images/documents/surveys/Industries_Survey/Industries_Survey_2009/survey0/data/Doc/Reports/LMMIS_2009-2010%20Report.pdf

Central Statistics Agency (CSA, 2010). Report on Large and Medium Scale Manufacturing and Electricity Industry Survey. Addis Ababa November 2010

Charlotta, G., Soledad, N., and Sylaja, S. (2006). Productivity Growth, Adjustment Costs and Variable Factor Utilisation: the UK Case. Bank of England *Working Paper*, No. 295,

Chen, J. J. (2004). Determinants of Capital Structure of Chinese Listed Companies. *Journal of Business Research*, 57(12), *p*. 1341-1351.

Chikolwa, B. (2009). Investigating the Capital Structure of A-REITs. In *15th Pacific Rim Real Estate Society Conference, Sydney, Australia*.

Christopoulos, D., and Tsionas, E. (2004). "Financial Development and Economic Growth: Evidence from Panel Unit Root and Cointegration Tests." Journal of Development Economics 73, *p*. 55-74.

Coe, R., Stern, R., Allan, E., Beniest, J., and Awimbo, J. (2002). Data Analysis of Agroforestry Experiments. World Agroforestry Centre. Availableat: http://www.reading.ac.uk/ssc/n/resources/Docs/Data AnalysisOfAgroforestryExperiments-Part2.pdf. Date accessed: 12/09/2013.

Cohen, W. A. (1989). The Entrepreneur and Small Business Financial Problem Solver, John Wiley & Sons, New York.

Claessens, S., Honohan, P., and Co-chairs, R. L (2009). Policy Principles for Expanding Financial Access. Report of the CGD Task Force on Access to Financial Services. Centers for Global Development. Independent Research & Practical Ideas for Global Prosperity

Collier, P., Gunning, W. J., Ndulu, J. B., Stephen, A., and O'Connell, A. S. (2008) Harnessing Growth Opportunities: How Africa can Advance. *The Political Economy of Economic*

Collis, J., and Hussey, R. (2003). Business Research: A Practical Guide for Undergraduate and Postgraduate Students, second edition. Basingstoke: Palgrave Macmillan.

Commission on Legal Empowerment of the Poor (HLCLEP) paper (2006). Background issue paper on Legal Empowerment of the Poor Entrepreneurship;

Cowling, M., Liu, W., and Ledger, A. (2012). Small Business Financing in the UK before and During the Current Financial Crisis. *International Small Business Journal*, 30(7), *p*. 778-800.

Cramer, D. (1994). Introducing Statistics for Social Research: Step-by-Step Calculations and Computer Techniques Using SPSS. Routledge, London and New York.

Cressy, R. (1995). Business Borrowing and Control: A Theory of Entrepreneurial Types. *Small Business Economics,* 7, *p.* 291-300.

Creswell, J. W. (2009). Mapping the Field of Mixed Methods Research. Journal of Mixed Methods Research, 3, *p.* 95-108.

Dahmen, P., and Rodríguez, E. (2014). "Financial Literacy and the Success of Small Businesses: An Observation from a Small Business Development Centre," Numeracy: Vol. 7: Iss. 1, Article 3. DOI: http://dx.doi.org/10.5038/1936-4660.7.1.3

Dalberg. (2011). Report on Support to SMEs in Developing Countries through Financial Intermediaries: Dalberg Global Development Advisors

Damian, H., and David, C. (2007). Innovative Methodologies in Enterprise Research. United Kingdom: *Edward Elgar Publishing.*

Daskalakis, N., and Psillaki, M. (2008). Does Country or Firm Factors Explain Capital Structure? Evidence from SMEs in France and Greece. *Applied Financial Economics*, 18(2), *p.* 87-97.

Deakins, D., North, D., Baldock, R., and Whittam, G. (2008). SMEs' Access to Finance: Is there still a debt finance gap? *Institute for Small Business & Entrepreneurship*. 5-7 November 2008 Belfast, N. Ireland

Debonnet, G., Melamari, L., and Bomhard, B. (2006). Reactive Monitoring Mission to Simien Mountains National Park Ethiopia 10-17 May 2006. Joint World Heritage Centre-IUCN Monitoring Mission to Simien Mountains National Park World Heritage Property

Deesomsak, R., Krishna, P., and Pescetto, G. (2004). The Determinants of Capital Structure: Evidence from the Asia Pacific region. *Journal of Multinational Financial Management,* 14, *p.* 387-405.

Degefe, B. (1986). Survey of the Major Industrial Law in Ethiopia. A paper Submitted to the National Symposium on Industrial Development in Ethiopia.

Degryse, H., De Goeij, P., and Kappert, P. (2009). The Impact of Firm and Industry Characteristics on Small Firms'

Capital Structure: *Evidence from Dutch panel data*. Tilburg University.

Demeke M., Guta, F., and Ferede, T. (2006). Towards a More Employment-Intensive and Proper Economic Growth in Ethiopia: Issues and policies. Issues in Employment and Poverty Discussion Paper 22. Geneva: Employment Strategy Department, *International Labour Organization.*

Demirguk – Kunt. (2006). Finance and Development Choices for Developing Countries, World Bank Policy Research Working Paper 3955, June 2006.

Desta, A. (2010a). Microcredit for Poverty Alleviation and Fostering Environmentally Sustainable Development: A Review of African Case Studies, *International Journal of Business Research.* Vol. 10, No. 2, 2010.

Desta, A. (2010b). "Transitional Democratic Governance and Economic Development. The Ethiopian Experience." http:// tigraionline.com/democratic_ governance.html

Dimerguk – Kunt and Detragiache. (1998). Financial Liberalization and Financial Fragility, IMF Working Paper 98/83.

Dimetridas and Luintle (1997). The Direct Costs of Financial Repression; Evidence from India, May 1997, *The Review of Economics and Statistics*, Vol. 79, No. 2, *p.* 311-320

Dinh, H. T., Mavridis, D. A., and Nguyen, H. B. (2010). The Binding Constraint on Firms' Growth in Developing Countries. *World Bank Policy Research Working.* Paper Series No 5485.

Dixon, W. J., and Massey, F. J. (1983). *Introduction to Statistical Analysis.* 4th ed. New York: McGraw–Hill.

Donaldson, G. (1961). Corporate Debt Capacity: *A study of corporate debt policy and the determination of corporate debt capacity.* MA Dissertation, Boston: Harvard University.

Du, J., Lu, Y. and Tao, Z., (2012). "Bank Loans versus Trade Credit: Evidence from China" *Economics of Transition,* Vol. 20, Issue 3, *p.* 457-480.

du Plooy, G. (2009). Communication Research: Techniques, Methods and Applications. Cape Town: Juta & Co.

Ebashi, M., Sakai, H., and Takada, N. (1997). Development Policy on SMEs and Supporting Industries in Vietnam.

Edmister, R. O. (1970), Financial Ratios as Discriminant Predictors of Small Business Failure, Doctoral dissertation, The Ohio State University.

Eduardo, L., and Pages, C. (2011). "Face-to-Face with Productivity," *Finance and Development*, 48(1), *p.* 16-19.

Emecheta, C. B., and Ibe, C. R. (2014). Impact of Bank Credit on Economic Growth in Nigeria: Application of Reduced Vector Autoregressive (VAR) Technique. *European Journal of Accounting Auditing and Finance Research* Vol.2, No.9, *p.*11-21

Eriotis, N., Vasiliou, D., and Ventoura-Neokosmidi, Z. (2007). How Firm Characteristics Affect Capital Structure: An Empirical Study. *Managerial Finance*, 33(5), *p.* 321-331.

Esperança, J. P., Gama, A. P. M., and Gulamhussen, M. A. (2003). Corporate Debt Policy of Small Firms: An Empirical (re) Examination. *Journal of Small Business and Enterprise Development*, 10(1), *p.* 62-80.

Ethiopian Economic Association (EEA, 2015). Small and Micro Enterprises (SMEs) Development in Ethiopia: Policies, Performances, Constraints and Prospects. *EEA Research Brief.* Issue No. 5, February 2015.

European Commission (2006). EU SME Definition, 6 May Doc (2003) 1442. Available online at:http://ec.europa.eu/enterprise//enterprise_policy/sme_definition/index_en.htm. Retrieved 29/5/15.

Fadejeva, L., and Melihous, A. (2009). Measuring Factor Productivity and Variables Factor Utilization: Sector Approach, the Case of Lativia.

Fagan, M. and Zhao, S. (2009). SME financing in China: The current situation, problems and possible solutions. *International Journal of Entrepreneurship and Small Business,* 8(2), *p.* 171-185.

Fama E., and French K. (2002). Testing Trade-off and Pecking Order Predictions About Dividends and Debt. *Review of Financial Studies,* 15, *p.* 1-33.

Fanta, B. A. (2012). Banking reform and SME financing in Ethiopia: Evidence from the manufacturing sector. African Journal of Business Management Vol. 6(19), *p.* 6057-6069, Available online at http://www.academicjournals.org/AJBM

Fattouh, B., Scaramozzino, P., and Harris, L. (2005). Capital structure in South Korea: A Quantile Regression Approach. *Journal of Development Economics*, 76(1), *p.* 231-250.

Fazzari, S. M., Hubbard, R. G., and Petersen, C. B. (2000). Financing Constraints and Corporate Investment: Response to Kaplan and Zingales. *Quarterly Journal of Economics,* 115(2), *p.* 695-705

Fazzari, S. M., Hubbard, G. R., and Petersen, C. B. (1988). Financing Constraints and Corporate Investment," *Brookings Papers on Economic Activity*, 1: *p.* 141-195.

Fazzari, S. M., Hubbard, G. R and Petersen, C. B. (2000). Investment-Cash Flow Sensitivities are Useful: A Comment on Kaplan and Zingales, Quarterly Journal of Economics 115, *p.* 695-705.

Fischer, E. O., Heinkel, R., and Zechner, J. (1989). Dynamic Capital Structure Choice: Theory and Tests. *The Journal of Finance.* 44(1), *p.* 19-40.

Felipe, J., and Adams, G. F. (2005). "A theory of Production" The Estimation of The Cobb-Dauglas Function: A Retrospective View. *Eastern Economic Journal*, Vol. 31, No. 3, Summer 2005

Fluck, Z., Holtz-Eakin, D., and Rosen, H. S. (1998). Where Does the Money Come From? *The financing of small entrepreneurial enterprises*, Occasional Paper 191. Centre for Policy Research, Maxwell School of Citizenship and Public Affairs: Syracuse University.

Frank, Z. M., and Goyal, K. V (2005). Trade-off and Pecking Order Theories of Debt. Central for Corporate Governance. *Working Paper and Handbook of Corporate Finance*: Empirical Corporate Finance

Frank, M. Z., and Goyal, V. K. (2009). Capital Structure Decisions: Which Factors are Reliably Important?. *Financial Management*, 38(1), *p.* 1-37.

Frydenberg, S. (2001). The Importance of Being Indebted. *Working Paper*, Trondheim Business School, *p.* 1-29.

Fu, T. W., Ke, M. C., and Huang, Y. S. (2002). Capital Growth, Financing Source and Profitability of Small Businesses: Evidence from Taiwan Small Enterprises. *Small Business Economics*, 18(4), *p.* 257-267.

Fuchs, M. L., Iacovone, T., Jaeggi, M., Napier, R., Pearson, G. P., and Sanchez. C. V. (2011). Financing Small and Medium Enterprises in the Republic of South Africa. *World Bank*. Washington, DC.

Gatti, R. and Love, I. (2006): Does Access to Credit Improve Productivity? Evidence From Bulgarian Firms. World Bank Development Research Group. *Policy research working paper 3921*. World Bank

Gaud, P., Jani, E., Hoesli, M., and Bender, A. (2005). The Capital Structure of Swiss Companies: An Empirical Analysis Using Dynamic Panel Data. *European Financial Management*, 11(1), *p.* 51-69.

Gebreeyesus, M. (2008). Firm Turnover and Productivity Differentials in Ethiopian Manufacturing Industry: *Journal of Productivity Analysis 29, p.*113-129

Gebrehiwot, A., and Wolday, A. (2006). Micro and Small Enterprises (MSEs) in Ethiopia: Empirical Evidence. *Eastern Africa Social Science Research Review*, 22 (1): 63-86

Geda, A. (2006). The Structure and Performance of Ethiopia's Financial Sector in the Pre- and Post-Reform Period with a Special Focus on Banking. *World Institute for Development Economic Research*. Research Paper No. 2006/112

Ghani, E., and Suri, V. (1999). "Productivity Growth, Capital Accumulation, and the Banking Sector: Some Lessons from Malaysia," *The World Bank Policy Research Working Paper Series*: 2252.

Ghosh, S. (2006). East Asian Finance: The Road to Robust Markets. *The World Bank*, Washington, DC.

Gill, J., and Johnson, P. (1997). Research Methods for Manager (2nd edition), London: Paul Chapman

Giorno, C., Richardson, P., Roseveare. D., and Noord, P. V. (1995). Estimating Potential Output, Output Gaps and Structural Budget Balances. OECD, *Working Paper*, no. 152.

Government of the Federal Democratic Republic of Ethiopia (FDRoE, 2011), Micro and Small Enterprise Development Strategy, provision framework and methods of Implementation.

Gmecheta, C. B., and Ibe, C. R. (2014). Impact of Bank Credit on Economic Growth in Nigeria: Application of Reduced Vector Autoregressive (VAR) Technique. *European Journal of Accounting Auditing and Finance Research. Vol.2, No.9, p.11-21*

Graham, J. R., and Leary, M. T. (2011). A Review of Empirical Capital Structure Research and Directions for the Future. *Annual Review Financial Economic*, 3(1), *p*. 309-345.

Green, C., Kimuyu, P., Mannos, R. and Murinde, V., (2002). "How Do Small Firms in Developing Countries Raise Capital? Evidence from a Large-Scale Survey of Kenyan Micro and Small Enterprises." *Economic Research Paper* No. 02/6, Department of Economics, Loughborough University, UK.

Gregory, B. T., Rutherford, M. W., Oswald, S., and Gardiner, L. (2005). An Empirical Investigation of the Gcycle Theory of Small firm Financing. *Journal of Small Business Management*, 43(4), 382-392

Grifell-Tatjé, E., and Lovell, C. A. K. (1996). Profits and Productivity. The Wharton Financial Institutions Centre. *The Working Paper Series*

Growth in Africa, 1960- 2000 (V-I): in Ndulu, B. O'Connell, S., Bates, R, Collier, P. and Soludo C. (eds). Cambridge University Press

Guariglia, A., Xiaoxuan, L., and Lina, S. (2008). "Internal Finance and Growth: Micro- Econometric Evidence on Chinese Firms," *IZA Discussion Papers 3808*, Institute for the Study of Labor (IZA).

Hadlock, C. J., and James, C. M. (2002). Do Banks Provide Financial Slack?. *The Journal of Finance*, 57(3), *p.* 1383-1419.

Hall, G.C., Hutchinson, P.J., and Nicos, M. (2004). Determinants of the Capital Structures of European SMEs. *Journal of Business Finance and Accounting,* 31(5 and 6), *p.* 711–728.

Hall, G., Hutchinson, P., and Michaelas, N. (2000). Industry Effects on the Determinants of Unquoted SMEs' Capital Structure. *International Journal of the Economics of Business*, 7(3), *p.* 297-312.

Hamilton, L. C. (2013). *Statistics with Stata: Updated for Version 12.* 8th ed. Boston: Brooks/Cole

Hansson, G. H. (2004). Ethiopia: Economic Performance and the Role of the Private Sector. *Country Economic Report* 2004:4

Hansson, G. (2001) "Ethiopian reforms: government legitimacy, economic growth and development" in M. Lundahl (ed) *From Crisis to Growth in Africa?*, London and New York: Routledge

Hansson, G. H. (1998). "Ethiopia: Regional and Business Sector Challenges" *country Economic Report 1998:3,* Stockholm: Sida

Hansson, G. H. (1995). The Ethiopian Economy 1974-94: *Ethiopia Tikdem and After,* London and New York: Routledge

Heitor, A., and Campello, M (2001). Financial Constraints and Investment-cash flow Sensitivities: New Research Directions, *working paper*, New York University.

Henze, E. P. (2004). Layers of Time: A History of Ethiopia. Third Edition. First Published United States of America in 2000.

Hepburn, C., and Baptist, S. (2012). Intermediate Inputs and Economic Productivity. Centre for Climate Change *Economics and Policy Working Paper No.* 112 and Grantham Research Institute on Climate Change and the Environment Working Paper No. 95

Hodgman, D. (1962). "Reply", Quarterly *Journal of Economics*, 76, 488^93

Hodgman, D. (1960). "Credit Risk and Credit Rationing", Quarterly Journal of Economics, 74, *p.* 258-278.

Holmes S., and Kent, P. (1991). An Empirical Analysis of the Financial Structure of Small and Large Australian Manufacturing Enterprises. *Journal of Small Business Finance*, 1(2), *p.* 141-154.

Hoshi, T., and Kashyap, A. (2004). "Japan's Financial Crisis and Economic Stagnation." *Journal of Economic Perspectives* 18, *p.* 3-26.

Hovakimian, A., Hovakimian, G., and Tehranian, H. (2004). Determinants of Target Capital Structure: The Case of Dual Debt and Equity Issues. *Journal of Financial Economics*, 71(3), *p.* 517-540.

Hovakimian, A., Opler, T. and Titman, S. (2001). The Debt-Equity Choice. *Journal of Financial and Quantitative Analysis*, 36(1), *p.* 1-24.

Hutchinson, P., (2003). How Much Does Growth Determine SMEs' Capital Structure?. *16th Annual Conference of Small Enterprise Association of Australia and New Zealand.*

Hutchinson, P., and Meric, I., Meric, G. (1988). The Financial Characteristics of Small Firms Which Achieve Quotation on the UK Unlisted Securities Market, *Journal of Business Finance & Accounting,* 15(1)

Ibrahim, H., and Masron, T. A. (2011). Capital Structure and the Firm determinants: Evidence from Small and Medium Enterprises (SMEs) in Malaysia. *International Proceedings of Economics Development and Research*, 7.

Ibarraran, P., Maffioli, A., and Stucchi, R. (2009). "SME Policy and Firm's Productivity in Latin America" Discussion Paper No. 4486. Institute for the Study of Laobour (IZA), Germany.

Jaggi, B., and Considine, J. (1990). Differences in Financial Characteristics of Owner Controlled and Non-owner Controlled Acquired Firms, The Mid-Atlantic *Journal of Business, 26(2).*

Jen, F. C. (1963). The Determinants of the Degree of Insufficiency of Bank Credit to Small Business, *Journal of Finance,* 18, *p.* 694 - 695.

Jensen, M. (1986). Agency Costs of Free Cash Flow, Corporate Finance and Takeovers. *American Economic Review,* 76(2), *p.* 323-339.

Jensen, M. C., and Meckling, W. H. (1976). Theory of the Firm: Managerial Behaviour, Agency Costs and Ownership Structure. *Journal of Financial Economics*, 3(4), *p.* 305-360.

Jensen, M. (1986). Agency costs of free cash flow, corporate finance and takeovers. *American Economic Review,* 76(2), *p.* 323 -339.

Kahsay, T. H. (2013). Financial Development and Economic Growth Nexus: Evidence from Ethiopia (Johnson Approach to Co-Integration)

Kaplan, S. N., and Zingales, L. (2000). Investment-cash flow sensitivities are not valid measures of financing constraints, *Quarterly Journal of Economics* 115, *p.* 707-712

Karadeniz, E., Kandir, S. Y., Balcilar, M., and Onal, Y. B. (2009). Determinants of Capital Structure: Evidence from Turkish lodging companies. *International Journal of Contemporary Hospitality Management*, 21(5), *p.* 594-609.

Kayanula, D., and Quartey, P. (2000). The Policy Environment for Promoting Small and Medium Sized Enterprises in Ghana and Malawi. *Finance and Development Working Paper Series Paper No 15*. Institute for Development Policy and Management, University of Manchester, Manchester

Keasey, K., and Watson, R. (1991). The State of the Art of Small Firm Failure Prediction: Achievements and Prognosis" *International Small Business Journal.* 9(4): *p.* 11-29.

Keatinge, T. (2014). The Role of Public and Private Sector Banking in Ethiopia's Future Economic Growth. *Global Centre Policy Brief.*

Kemsley, D., and Nissim, D. (2002). Valuation of the Debt Tax Shield. *The Journal of Finance*, 57(5), *p.* 2045-073.

Kerr, W. R., and Nanda, R. (2009). Democratizing Entry: Banking Deregulations, Financing Constraints, and Entrepreneurship. *Journal of Financial Economics* 94: *p.* 124.49.

Khandker, S., Samad, H. A., and Ali, R. (2013). Does Access to Finance Matter in Microenterprise Growth? Evidence from Bangladesh. Evidence from Bangladesh. *World Bank Policy Research Working Paper* (6333).

Kirchhoff, B. A., and Kirchhoff, J. J. (1987). Family Contribution to Productivity and Profitability in Small Businesses, *Journal of Small Business Management*, p. 25

Kiyota, Peitsch and Stern (2007). The Case for Financial Sector Liberalization in Ethiopia, Gerald Ford School of Public Policy, University of Michigan, *Discussion Paper* No.565

Klapper, L. F., Sarria-Allende, V., and Zaidi, R. (2006). Firm-level analysis of small and medium size enterprise financing in Poland. *World Bank Policy Research Working Paper 3984,* Washington: World Bank.

Klassen, L. H., Koych, L.M., and Witteveen H. J. (eds). (1959). Jan Tinbergen Selected Papers. Amsterdam: North Holland; (1959): *p.* 1982-1221.

Kletzer, M. K. (2004). Liberalizing Capital Flows in India: Financial Repression, Macroeconomic Policy, and Gradual Reforms. Indian Policy Forum, 2004

Knox, K. (2004). A Researcher's Dilemma - Philosophical and Methodological Pluralism. Electronic Journal of Business Research Methods 2(2): *p*. 119-128.

Krishnan, V. S., and Moyer, R. C. (1996). Determinants of Capital Structure: An Empirical Analysis of Firms in Industrialized Countries. *Managerial Finance*, 22(2), *p*. 39-55.

Kuntchev,V., Ramalho, R., Jorge Rodríguez-Meza, J., and. Yang, S. J. (2012). "What have we learned from the Enterprise Surveys regarding access to finance by SMEs?" *Enterprise Analysis Unit of the World Bank Group*. Available at: http://www.enterprisesurveys.org/ Research

Kushnir, K., Mirmulstein, L. M., and Ramalho, R. (2010). Micro, Small, and Medium Enterprises around the World: How Many Are There, and What Affects the Count?

Laitinen, E. K. (1992). Financial processes In Newly-Founded Firms, *International Small Business Journal,* 10(4), *p*. 47-54.

Lanjouw, J. O., and Lanjouw, P. (2001). The Rural non-farm Sector: Issues and Evidence from Developing Countries. *Agricultural Economics,* 26: *p*. 1-23. doi: 10.1111/j.1574-0862.2001.tb00051.x

Lashitew, A. A. (2011). Does Access to Finance Lower Firms' Cost of Capital? Empirical Evidence from International Manufacturing Data Research Memorandum GD-120.

Leech, N. L., Barrett, K. C., and Morgan, G. A. (2005). *SPSS for intermediate statistics: Use and interpretation*. Psychology Press.

Le, N. T. B., and Nguyen, T. V. (2009). The Impact of Networking on Bank Financing: The Case of Small and Medium-sized Enterprises in Vietnam. *Entrepreneurship, Theory and Practice,* 33(4), *p*. 867-887.

Lewis-Beck, S. M. (1974). Determining the Importance of an Independent Variable: A Path Analytic Solution. Social Science Research 3, *p.* 95-107

Lev, B. (1983). Some Economic Determinants of Time Series Properties of Earnings. *Journal of Accounting and Economics, 5.*

Levine (2001). "International Financial Liberalization and Economic Growth." *Review of International Economics* 9(4): *p.* 688-702.

Levinsohn, J., and Petrin, A. (2000). Estimating Production Functions Using Inputs to Control for Unobservables. *NBER Working Paper* No.7819,

Li, K., Yue, H., and Zhao, L. (2009). Ownership, Institutions, and Capital Structure: Evidence from China. *Journal of Comparative Economics,* 37(3), *p.* 471-490.

Lora, E., and Pagés, C. (2011). "Face-to-Face with Productivity," Finance and Development, 48(1), *p.* 16-19.

López-Gracia, J., and Sánchez-Andújar, S. (2007). Financial Structure of the Family Business: Evidence from a group of small Spanish firms. *Family Business Review,* 20(4), *p.* 269-287.

Love, I. (2003). Financial Development and Financing Constraints: International Evidence from the Structural Investment Model." Review of Financial Studies 16(3): *p.* 765–91.

Love. I., and Zicchino. L. (2006). Financial Development and Dynamic Investment Behaviour: Evidence from panel VAR Inessa. *World Bank, Research Department—Finance Group.* The Quarterly Review of Economics and Finance 46 (2006), *p.* 190–210

Lucas, R. E. (1988). On the Mechanics of Economic Development". *Journal of Monetary Economics* 22, *p.* 3–42.

Mac An Bhaird, C., and Lucey, B. (2006). What Determines the Capital Structure of SMEs: Irish evidence? *Working*

Paper, Dublin City University and Trinity College Dublin.

Majumdar, K. S. (1997). The Impact of Size and Age on Firm-Level Performance: Some Evidence from India. *Review of Industrial Organization* 12: *p.* 231-241, 1997. Kluwer Academic Publishers

Malesky, E. J., and Taussig, M. (2009). Where Is Credit Due? Legal Institutions, Connections, and the Efficiency of Bank Lending in Vietnam. *Journal of Law, Economics, and Organization,* 25(2), *p.* 535-578. doi: http://dx.doi.org/10.1093/jleo/ewn011

Mammo, M. (2008). Network of Ethiopian Scholars (NES). Commentary No.17.

Marcus, G. H. (2002). A History of Ethiopia. University of California press. Updated edition (2002)

Margaret E. S. (2003). Models of Firm Profitability. *Journal of Economic Literature* classification numbers: D43, G13, L13, L71. University of Warwick Coventry CV4 7AL UK

Mario, V. B. (2015). Bank Credit and Productivity: Evidence from Mexican Firms. *Working Papers*

Matsaganis, M., and Flevotomou, M. (2010). Distributional Implications of tax Evasion in Greece. Retrieved: 22, 03, 2011,fromhttp://www.ecineq.org/ecineq_ba/papers/Matsaganis.pdf

McDonald, J. (1999). The Determinants on Firm Profitability in Australia manufacturing, *The Economic Record,* Vo.75 No.229, *p.* 115-126

McKinnon, R. I. (1973). Money and Capital in Economic Development, Washington, DC: Brookings Institution.

McMahon, R., and Stanger, A. (1995). Understanding the Small Business Enterprise Financial Objective Function. *Entrepreneurship: Theory and Practice*, 19(4), *p.* 21-39

McMahon, R., Holmes, P., Hutchinson, P., and Forsaith, D. (1993). *Small Enterprise Financial Management:* Theory and Practice, Harcourt Brace, Sydney.

Meric I., and Meric G., (1992), A Comparison of the Financial Characteristics of Listed and Unlisted Companies, *Midwestern Journal of Business and Economics,* 7(1), *p.*19-31.

Meric, I., Ross, L. W., Weidman, S. M., and Meric, G. (1997). A Comparison of the Financial Characteristics of U.S. and Japanese Chemical Firms, *Multinational Business Review, p.* 23 -27.

Michaelas, N., Chittenden, F., and Poutziouris, P. (1999). Financial Policy and Capital Structure Choice in UK SMEs: Empirical evidence from company panel data. *Small Business Economics*, 12(2), *p.* 113-130.

Miller, H. M. (1998). Financial Markets and Economic Growth. *Journal of Applied Corporate Finance* Volume 11, Issue 3, *p.* 8-15,

Ministry of Finance and Economic Development (MoFED, 2014). Growth and Transformation Plan Annual Progress Report for F.Y 2012/2013. Addis Ababa

Ministry of Urban Development and Construction (MoUDC, 2013). Survey on Micro and Small Enterprises (MSEs) in Selected Major Cities of Ethiopia. p. 28

Ministry of Finance and Economic Development (MoFED, 2012). Assessing Progress towards the Millennium Development Goals. Ethiopian MDGs Report 2012. United Nations Country Team Ethiopia.

Ministry of Finance and Economic Development (MoFED, 2011a). Annual Report on Macroeconomic Development in Ethiopia

Ministry of Finance and Economic Development (MoFED, 2011b). Growth and Transformation Plan 2010/11-2014/15 Volume I and II, Addis Ababa, November.

Ministry of Finance & Economic Development (MoFED, 2011c). The Federal Democratic Republic of Ethiopia.

Growth and Transformation Plan (GTP) 2010/11-2014/15

Ministry of Finance and Economic Development (MoFED, 2010). Growth and Transformation Plan (GTP) 2010/11-2014/15. The Federal Democratic Republic of Ethiopia September 2010 Addis Ababa

Ministry of Finance and Economic Development (MoFED, 2003). Ethiopia: Sustainable Development and Poverty Reduction Program (SDPRP), December 2003, Addis Ababa: Ministry of Finance and Economic Development

Ministry of Trade and Industry (MoTI, 2004). Micro and Small Enterprises Development Strategy: the Federal Democratic Republic of Ethiopia Ministry of Trade and Industry: Addis Ababa

Modigliani, F., and Miller, M. (1958). The Cost of Capital, Corporation Finance and the Theory of Investment. *American Economic Review,* 48(3), *p.* 261-297.

Modigliani, F., and Miller, M. (1963). Corporate Income Taxes and the Cost of Capital: A Correction. *American Economic Review,* 53(3), *p.* 433-443.

Moller, L. C., and Wacker, K. M. (2015). Ethiopia's Growth Acceleration and How to Sustain It: Insights from a Cross-Country Regression Model. *World Bank, Washington, DC. https://openknowledge.worldbank.org/handle/10986/22164 License: CC BY 3.0 IGO."*

Montiel, J. P. (2003). Macroeconomics in Emerging Markets, 2003, *Cambridge University Press, p.* 187-307

Morgan, D. L. (2007). Paradigms Lost and Pragmatism Regained: Methodological Implications of Combining Qualitative and Quantitative Methods. *Journal of Mixed Methods Research 1(1): p.* 48-76.

Moreno, M., and Slootmaekers, V. (2008). The Missing Link between Financial Constraints and Productivity. *LICOS*

Centre for Institutions and Economic Performance: Discussion Paper, 208.

Moseley, F. (2012), "A Critique of the Marginal Productivity Theory of the Price of Capital", real-world economics review, issue no. 59, 12 March 2012, *p.* 131-137, http://www.paecon.net/PAEReview/issue59/Moseley 59.pdf

Moyi, E., (2013). "Credit and Employment Growth among Small enterprise in Kenya." *International Journal of Business and Economics Research,* Vol. 2, No. 3 *p.* 69-76.

Murthy and Bhojanna (2008). Business Research Method 2nd Edition.

Myers, S. C., and Rajan., R. G. (1998), "The Paradox of Liquidity", *Quarterly Journal of Economics,* Vol. 113, No. 3, p. 733-71.

Myers, S. C., and Majluf, N. (1984). Corporate Financing and Investment Decisions when Firms have Information those Investors do not have. *Journal of Financial Economics,* 13, *p.* 187-224.

Myers, S.C. (1984). The Capital Structure Puzzle. *Journal of Finance,* 39, *p.* 575-592.

Myers, S. C. (1977). Determinants of Corporate Borrowing. *Journal of Financial Economics*, 5(2), *p.* 147-175.

Nagler. P., and Naudé. W. (2014). Labour Productivity in Rural African Enterprises: Empirical Evidence from the LSMS-ISA. *Discussion Paper* No. 8524

National Bank of Ethiopia (NBE, 2011). Licensing and Supervision of Banking Business Minimum Capital Requirement. Directive Number SBB/50/2011.

Nenadic, O., and Zucchini, W. (2004). Statistical Analysis with R. A quick start

Neuman, W. L. (2006). Social Research Methods: Qualitative and Quantitative Approaches (6th ed.). Boston: Pearson Education.

Neusser, K., and Kugler, M. (1998). Manufacturing Growth and Financial Development: Evidence from OECD

Countries. The MIT Press Stable. *The Review of Economics and Statistics,* Vol. 80, No. 4 (Nov., 1998), pp. 638-646: URL: http://www.jstor.org/stable/2646845 Accessed: 01-10-2015 16:43 UTC

Newman, A., Gunessee, S., and Hilton, B. (2011). Applicability of Financial Theories of Capital Structure to the Chinese Cultural Context: A Study of Privately Owned SMEs. *International Small Business Journal,*

Newman, A. (2010). Capital Structure Determinants of Private Small and Medium-sized Enterprises in China. Doctoral dissertation, University of Nottingham

Newman, A. (2010). Capital Structure Determinants of Private Small and Medium-sized Enterprises in China. Doctoral dissertation, University of Nottingham.

Ng, S. I., Lee, J. A., and Soutar, G. N. (2007). Are Hofstede's and Schwartz's value frameworks congruent?. *International Marketing Review*, 24(2), *p.* 164-180.

Nguyen, T. D. K., and Ramachandran, N. (2006). Capital Structure in Small and Medium-Sized Enterprises: The Case of Vietnam. *ASEAN Economic Bulletin,* 23(2), *p.* 192-211.

Nichter, S., and Goldmark, L. (2009). Small Firm Growth in Developing Countries. World Development Vol. 37, No. 9, p. 1453-1464

Nkurunziza, J., (2010). "The Effect of Credit on Growth and Convergence of Firm Size in Kenyan Manufacturing." *Journal of International Trade and Economic Development*, 19:3, pp. 465-494.

Organization for Economic Co-operation and Development (OECD, 2010). Policy Framework for Effective and Efficient Financial Regulation. General guidance and high-level checklist.

Olley, G., and Pakes, A. (1996). "The Dynamics of Productivity in the Telecommunications Equipment Industry," Econometrical, vol. 64, p. 1263-1279.

Olutunla, G. T., and Obamuyi, T. M. (2008): An Empirical Analysis of Factors Associated with the Profitability of Small and Medium Enterprises in Nigeria. *African Journal of Business Management* Vol.2 (x), *p.* 195-200, http://www.academicjournals.org/AJBM

Onwuegbuzie, J. A., and Collins, T. M. K. (2007). A Typology of Mixed Methods Sampling Designs in Social Science Research. The Qualitative Report Volume 12, p. 281-316 http://www.nova.edu/ssss/QR/QR12-2/onwuegbuzie2.pdf

Ooi, J. (1999). The Determinants of Capital Structure Evidence on UK Property Companies. *Journal of Property Investment and Finance*, 17(5), p. 464-480.

Ortqrist, D., Eryadi, K., Mosli, Rahman, S., and Selavarajah, C. (2006). Determinants of Capital Structure in New Ventures: Evidence from Swedish Longitudinal Data. *Journal of Development Entrepreneurship*, 11(4), *p.* 277-296.

Osei-Assibey, E. (2013). Source of Finance and Small Enterprise's Productivity Growth in Ghana. *African Journal of Economic and Management Studies*, 4(3), *p.* 372-386.

Ou, C., and Haynes, G. W. (2006). Acquisition of additional equity capital by small firm: Findings from the National Survey of Small Business Finances. *Small Business Economics*, 27(2-3), *p.* 157-168.

Ozkan, A. (2001). Determinants of Capital Structure and Adjustment to Long Run Target: Evidence from UK Company Panel Data. *Journal of Business Finance and Accounting*, 28(1-2), p. 175-198.

Pallant, J. (2011). SPSS Survival Manual: A Step by Step Guide to Data Analysis Using SPSS (4th edition). Allen & Unwin, Crow's Nest NSW.

Pandula, G. (2011). An Empirical Investigation of Small and Medium Enterprises' Access to Bank Finance: The case of an Emerging Economy.

Pandey, I. M. (2001). Capital Structure and the Firm Characteristics: Evidence from an emerging market. *Indian Institute of Management Ahmedabad Working Paper*, (2001-10), 04.

Panno, A. (2003). An Empirical Investigation on the Determinants of Capital Structure: The UK and Italian experience. *Applied Financial Economics*, 13(2),p. 97-112.

Patel, B. K., Muir-Leresche, K., Coe, R., and Hainsworth, D. S. (Eds.). (2004). The Green Book: A guide to effective Graduate research in African Agriculture, Environment, and Rural Development. Kampala, Uganda: The African Crop Science Society.

Pedharzur, E. J., and Schmelkin, L. P. (1991). Measurement, Design, and Analysis: An Integrated Approach, *Lawrence Erlbaum Associates*, Publishers.

Penrose, E. T. (1952). Biological Analogies in the Theory of the Firm. *The American Economic Review*, p. 804-819.

Pere, J. Montiel (2003), *Macroeconomics in Emerging Markets*, 2003, Cambridge University Press, *p*. 187-307.

Petersen, M. A., and Rajan, R. G. (2002). Does distance still matter? The Information Revolution in Small Business Lending. *The Journal of Finance*, 57(6), *p*. 2533-2570.

Petersen, R., and Schuman, J. (1987). Capital Structure of Growing Small Firms: A 12-country study on becoming bankable. *International Small Business Journal,* 5(4),10-22.

Pettit, R. R., and Singer, R. F. (1985). Small Business Finance: A research agenda. *Financial Management*, 14, p. 47-60.

Phillips, P. A., and Sipahioglu, M. A. (2004). Performance Implications of Capital Structure: Evidence from quoted UK organisations with hotel interests. *Service Industries Journal*, 24(5), *p*. 31-51.

Psillaki, M., and Daskalakis, N. (2009). Are The Determinants of Capital Structure Country or Firm Specific?. *Small Business Economics*, 33(3), *p*. 319-333.

Qian, Y., Tian, Y., and Wirjanto, T. (2009). Do publicly listed Chinese companies adjust their capital structure toward a target level?. *China Economic Review,* 20(4), *p.* 662-676.

Rahaman, M. M. (2011). Access to Financing and Firm Growth. *Journal of Banking & Finance* 35(2011), p. 709-723

Rajan, R. G. 2005. 'Has financial development made the world riskier?' Proceedings of the 2005 Jackson Hole Conference organized by the Kansas City Fed.

Rajan, R. G., and Zingales, L. (1995). What do We Know about Capital Structure? Some Evidence from International Data. *Journal of Finance*, 50(5), p. 1421-1460.

Reyes, A., Lensink, R., Kuyvenhoven, A., and Moll, H. (2012). Selected Poster prepared for presentation at the International Association of Agricultural Economists (IAAE) Triennial Conference, Foz do Iguaçu, Brazil, 18-24 August, 2012.

Rioja, F., and Valev, N. (2004). "Finance and the Sources of Growth at Various Stages of Economic Development," *Economic Inquiry*, Vol. 42, No.1, p. 127-140.

Riportella, C. C., and Martínez, J. C. (2003). What do We Know about the Financial Behaviour of the Spanish SMEs? An empirical analysis. *Business Economics, Series 08,* Universidad Carlos III de Madrid.

Robb, A., Consulting, M., San, C. L. L., and Rafael, C. A. (2012). Access to Capital Among Young Firms, Minority-Owned Firms, Women-Owned Firms, and High-Tech Firms. Under contract no. SBAHQ-11-M-0203.

Robb, A., and Robinson, D. (2012). The Capital Structure Decisions of New Firms, forthcoming, *Review of Financial Studies.*

Robin, B., and Pande, R. (2005) "Do Rural Banks Matter? Evidence from the indian social banking experiment." *The American economic review* 95 (3), *p.* 780-795.

Rocco, T. S., and Plakhotnik, M. S. (2009). Literature Reviews, Conceptual Frameworks, and Theoretical Frameworks:

Terms, Functions, and Distinctions. *Human Resource Development Review* 8(1), p. 120-130.

Romano, C. A., Tanewski, G. A., and Smyrnios, K. X. (2000). Capital Structure Decision Making: A model for family business. *Journal of Business Venturing*, 16, *p.* 285-310.

Ross, S. A., Westerfield, R. W., and Jaffe, J. (1999). *Corporate Finance*, 5th edition, Irwin and McRaw-Hill, Boston.

Ross, S. A. (1977). The Determination of Financial Structure: The Incentive Signaling Approach. *Bell Journal of Economics*, 8(1), *p.* 23-40.

Roubini and Sala-i-Martin (1991). Financial Repression and Economic Growth, November 1991, *Journal of Development Economics* 39 (1992) 5-30. North-Holland

Saarani, A. N., and Shahadan, F. (2013). The Determinant of Capital Structure of SMEs in Malaysia: Evidence from Enterprise 50 (e50) SMEs. *Asian Social Science*, 9(6), *p.* 64.

Saunders, M., Lewis, P., and Thornhill, A. (2009). *Research Methods for Business Students.* Harlow, England: Pearson Education.

Sayılgan, G., Karabacak, H., and Küçükkocaoğlu, G. (2006). The Firm-Specific Determinants of Corporate Capital Structure: Evidence from Turkish panel data. *Investment Management and Financial Innovations*, 3(3), *p.* 125-139.

Schreyer, P., Brandt, N., and Zipperer, V. (2015). Productivity Measurement with Natural Capital. *Society for Economic Measurement Annual Conference*

Scott, Jr. (1976). A Theory of Optimal Capital Structure. *The Bell Journal of Economics*, 7(1), p. 33-54.

Shariff, M. N., Peou, C., and Ali, J. (2010). "Moderating Effect of Government Policy on Entrepreneurship and Growth Performance of Small-Medium Enterprises in Cambodia." *International Journal of Business and Management Science* 3(1), p. 57.

Shariff, M. N., and Peou, C. (2008). "The Relationship of Entrepreneurial Values, Firm Financing and the Management and growth Performance of Small-

Medium Enterprises in Cambodia." *Problems and Perspectives in Management* Volume 6, Issue 4.

Shinozaki, S. (2012). A New Regime of SME Finance in Emerging Asia: Empowering Growth-Oriented SMEs to Build Resilient National Economies", ADB Working Paper Series on Regional Economic Integration, No. 104, available: http://www.aric.adb.org/pdf/workingpaper/WP104_Shinozaki_SME_Finance.pdf.

Siedschlag, I., Toole, C., Murphy, G., and Connell, B. (2014). Access to External Financing and Firm Growth. Background Study for the European Competitiveness Report 2014. Carried out for the European Commission within the Framework Contract ENTR/2009/033

Sisay, Y. (2008). Determinants of Smallholder Farmers' Access to Formal Credit: The case of Metema Worda, North Gonder, Ethiopia.

Skrepnek, H. G. (2004). Accounting- Versus Economic-Based Rates of Return: Implications for Profitability Measures in the Pharmaceutical Industry. The Centerfor *Health Outcomes and PharmacoEconomic Research,* College of Pharmacy, University of Arizona, Tucson, Arizona

Sleuwaegen, L., and Goedhuys, M. (2002). Growth of Firms in Developing Countries, Evidence from Cote d'Ivoire. *Journal of Development Economics,* Volume 68, Number 1, June 2002, p. 117-135(19)

Söderbom, M. (2012). "Firm Size and Structural Change: A Case Study of Ethiopia." *Journal African Economies,* Vol. 21, AERC Supplement 2, p. ii126–ii151

Sogorb-Mira, F. (2005). How SME uniqueness affects capital structure: Evidence from a 1994-1998 Spanish data panel. *Small business economics*, 25(5), p. 447-457.

Solow, R. (1957). Technical Change and the Aggregate Production Function", *Review of Economics and Statistics,* Vol. 39, p. 312-320

Stacks, D. W., and Salwen, M. B. (Eds.). (2009). An Integrated Approach to Communication Theory and Research (2nd ed.). New York: Routledge.

Stierwald, A. (2010). Determinants of Profitability: An Analysis of Large Australian Firms Melbourne Institute *Working Paper* No. 3/10

Stiglitz, J., and Weiss, A. (1983). "Incentive Effects of Terminations: Applications to Credit and Labour Markets". American Economic Review 73 (5), p. 912–927. Evidence from Malaysia, *Journal of Economic Development* 84(2007) p. 215-233

Stopher, P. (2012). Collecting, Managing, Assessing data Using Sample Surveys. Cambridge University Press, Cambridge

Syverson, C. (2011) What Determines Productivity? *Journal of Economic Literature* 2011, 49:2, 326–365. http:www.aeaweb.org/articles.php?doi=10.1257/jel.49.2.326

Tadesse, S. (2002). "Financial Architecture and Economic Performance: International Evidence." *Journal of Financial Intermediation* 11, p. 429-54.

Terziovski., and Mile. (2010). Innovation Practice and its Performance Implications in Small and Medium Enterprises (SMEs) in the Manufacturing Sector: A Resource-Based View. *Strategic Management Journal.* 31 (8): p. 892-902

Thong, J.Y.L. (1999). An Integrated Model of Information Systems Adoption in Small Business. *Journal of Management Information Systems*, 15(4), p. 187-214.

Timmons, J. A. (2004). New Venture Creation*: Entrepreneurship for the 21st century*. New York: McGraw-Hill.

Tinbergen, J. Z. T. (1942). Theorie der Langfristigen Wirtschaftsentwicklung. . Weltwirtsschaftliches Archiv, 55(1), p. 511-549 (translated as on the theory of trend movements.

Tirfe, K. (1994) "Privatization and Valuation of Public Enterprises" in Getachew Yoseph and Abdulhamid Bedri Kello (eds.) Problems and Prospects of Private Sector Development in Ethiopia, *Proceedings of the Third Annual Conference on the Ethiopian Economy,* August 1994, Addis Ababa

Tong, G., and Green, C. J. (2005). Pecking Order or Trade-off hypothesis? Evidence on the Capital Structure of Chinese Companies. *Applied Economics*, 37(19), 2179-2189.

Tornell, A., Westermann, F., and Martinez, L. (2004). "The Positive Link between Financial Liberalization Growth and Crises." *NBER Working Paper* 10293.

Tybout, R. J. (2000), Manufacturing Firms in Developing Countries: How Well Do They Do, and why? *Journal of Economic Literature*, 38, 7-40.

UNDP (2014). Country Economic Brief produced. United Nations Development Programme in Ethiopia. UNDP Ethiopia's Policy Advisory Unit

UNDP (2012). Transformation, Excellence and Action. United Nations Development Programme in Ethiopia. Annual report

United Nations Development Programs (UNDP, 2012). Entrepreneurship Development Program in Ethiopia. Addis Ababa Ethiopia June, 2012.

Usman, M. U. (2014). Determinants of capital structure: Empirical evidence from large taxpayer share companies in Ethiopia. *International Journal of Economics and Finance*, 6(1), *p.* 53-65.

Van der Wijst, D. (1989). *Financial Structure in Small Business: Theory, tests and applications.* Berlin: Springer-Verlag

Vartanian, T. P. (2011). Secondary data analysis, New York, NY: Oxford.

Vos, E., Yeh, A. J. Y., Carter, S., and Tagg, S. (2007). The Happy Story of Small Business Financing. *Journal of Banking and Finance*, 31(9), p. 2648-2672.

Vestal, M. T (2010) "Democratic Governance and Human Rights: How to Win Elections in Ethiopia', Presented at the Conference on Ethiopia and the Horn of Africa, 9-11 April 2010, http://www.ethiopianreview.com/content/27575 (accessed 25 January 2016)

Vos, E., Yeh, A. J. Y., Carter, S., and Tagg, S. (2007). The Happy Story of Small Business Financing. *Journal of Banking and Finance*, 31(9), 2648-2672.

Wampah, H. 2013. 'What does it take to Build a Stable and Efficient Financial Sector for Sustained Growth and Structural Transformation in Africa', Speech at DEGRP/ODI Conference. Forthcoming in Griffith-Jones and te Velde 2014.

Ward, G. (2006). IFACs Commitment to SMPs and SMEs. IFAC small and medium practices forum, Hong Kong, July 3, 2006.

Williamson, O. E. (1988). Corporate Finance and Corporate Governance. *The journal of finance*, 43(3), *p*. 567-591.

Wolf, S., (2007). "Encouraging Innovation for Productivity Growth in Africa." African Trade Policy Centre Working Paper No. 54, United Nations Economic Commission for Africa (UNECA). Addis Ababa, Ethiopia

Wondifraw, Z., Kibret, H., and Wakaiga, J. (2015). African Economic Outlook report in Ethiopia. AfDB, OECD, UNDP 2015

Worku, Z. (2013). Social Capital as a Differential of Long-term Survival in Small and Medium-sized Enterprises in Ethiopia. *Special Issue on the Ethiopian Economy* 5(1): p. 142-154.

World Bank (WB, 2015). SME Finance in Ethiopia: Addressing the Missing Middle Challenge.Washington,DC.©WorldBank.https://openknowledge.worldbank.org/handle/10986/21488 License: CC BY 3.0 IGO.

World Bank Group (WBG, 2015). Fourth Ethiopia Economic Update: Overcoming Constraints in the Manufacturing Sector. *Washington, DC. © World Bank. https://openknowledge.worldbank.org/handle/10986/22317 License: CC BY 3.0 IGO."*

World Bank (WB, 2014a). 'Third Ethiopia Economic Update: Strengthening Export Performance through Improved Competitiveness', Washington D.C

World Bank (WB, 2014b). SME Finance in Ethiopia: Addressing the Missing Middle Challenge. World Bank, Washington, DC.

World Bank (WB, 2013). Ethiopia - Second Economic Update: Laying the Foundation for Achieving Middle Income Status". Washington D.C.

World Bank (WB, 2011a). World Development Report 2011, Conflict, Security, and Development The. International Bank for Reconstruction and Development / the World Bank

World Bank (WB, 2011b). Africa Development Indicator. Web database

World Bank (WB, 2011b). Enterprises Survey Report and Ethiopia Country Profile, International Finance Corporation

World Bank Group (WBG, 2014). Third Ethiopian Economic Update. Strengthening Export Performance through Improved Competitiveness

World Bank and Development Bank (2009).World Economic Forum. The Africa Competitiveness Report, WEF: Geneva, World Bank: Washington, DC and AfDB: Tunis.

World Bank (WB, 2003), Determinants of Private Sector Growth in Ethiopia's Urban Industry: The Role of Investment Climate, May 6, 2003, DECRG/RPED, *World Bank in Collaboration with the Ethiopian Research Institute (EDRI)*, Washington DC: DECRG/RPED, The World Bank

World Bank (2001a). World Development Report. Washington: Oxford University Press.

World Bank (2001b). Global Public Policies and Programs: Implications for Financing and Evaluation Proceedings from a World Bank Workshop Edited by Christopher, D. G., Ferroni, M., & Mody, A (ed). The International Bank for Reconstruction and Development/THE WORLD BANK

World Bank (2001c). Making Small Business Lending Profitable Proceedings from the Global Conference on Credit Scoring April 2-3, 2001 • Washington, D.C. International Finance Corporation. Global Finance Markets Group, IFC.

Wurgler, J. (2000). Financial Markets and the Allocation of Capital. "*Journal of Financial Economics* 58(1–2):187–214

Xuegong, S., and Xueyan, L. (2011). Small and Medium Enterprises' Access to Finance in China', in Harvie, C., S. Oum, and D. Narjoko (eds.), Small and Medium Enterprises (SMEs) Access to Finance in Selected East Asian Economies. ERIA Research Project Report 2010-14, Jakarta: ERIA. p.351-384.

Yeasmin, S., and Rahman, K. F. (2012). Triangulation' Research Method as the Tool of Social Science Research. *BUP Journal* 1(1): p. 154-163.

Zhao, B., and Wijewardana, W. P. (2012). Financial Leverage, Firm Growth and Financial Strength: Evidence in Sri Lanka, *Journal of Asian Pacific Business Innovation and Technology Management,* 2, p. 13-22.

Zhenhui, X., and Sudeshna, P. (2011): Financial Development and Total Productivity: Evidence from Indian's manufacturing sector.

Zhou, P., Ang, W. B and Poh, L. K (2007). A Survey of data Envelopment Analysis in Energy and Environmental Studies. *European Journal of Operational Research* 189 (2008) 1-18

Zikmund, W. G. (1997). Business Research Methods. 7th edition.

Zou, H., and Xiao, J. Z. (2006). The financing behaviour of listed Chinese firms. *The British Accounting Review*, 38(3), *p*. 239-258.

Zwedu. A. G. (2014). Financial Inclusion, Regulation and Inclusive Growth in Ethiopia. Shaping Policy for Development. Working paper 408

APPENDICES

APPENDIX A: ETHIOPIAN ECONOMY

Table A.1: Percentage Distribution of GDP by Economic Activity (at Constant Prices)

Industry/Year	2001/02	2002/03	2003/04	2004/05	2005/06	2006/07	2007/08	2008/09	2009/10
Agriculture, Hunting and Forestry	49.1	44.9	47.0	47.4	47.1	46.1	44.6	43.1	42.0
Crop	28.8	24.6	27.6	29.3	30.2	30.0	29.2	28.2	27.8
Animal Farming and Hunting	15.0	14.8	14.3	13.5	12.7	12.2	11.8	11.5	11.0
Forestry	5.2	5.5	5.0	4.6	4.2	3.9	3.6	3.4	3.2
Fishing	0.0	0.0	0.0	0.0	0.0	0.0	0.0	0.0	0.0
Mining and Quarrying	0.5	0.5	0.5	0.4	0.4	0.3	0.3	0.4	0.5
Manufacturing	5.3	5.5	5.2	5.2	5.2	5.0	5.0	4.9	4.9
Large and Medium Scale Manufacturing	3.4	3.6	3.4	3.4	3.5	3.4	3.4	3.4	3.5
Hotels and Restaurants	2.2	2.4	2.3	2.3	2.4	2.8	3.1	3.4	3.9
Transport and Communications	5.2	5.9	5.7	6.1	5.8	5.6	5.6	5.6	5.8
Financial Intermediation	1.4	1.5	1.7	1.8	2.1	2.2	2.5	2.6	2.7
Real Estate, Renting and Business Activities	7.8	8.7	8.1	7.7	8.0	8.2	8.6	9.1	9.9

Public Administration and Defence	4.6	4.8	4.3	4.2	4.0	4.0	4.1	4.4	4.1
Education	2.5	2.8	2.8	2.8	2.8	3.0	3.1	3.2	3.4
Health and Social Work	0.9	0.9	0.9	1.0	1.0	1.0	1.0	1.1	1.1
Other Community , Social & Personal Services	1.8	1.9	1.8	1.7	1.7	1.6	1.6	1.6	1.5
Private Households with Employed Persons	0.3	0.3	0.3	0.3	0.2	0.2	0.2	0.2	0.2
GDP at Constant Market Prices	107.7	107.7	109.4	108.6	108.0	107.6	107.2	106.0	107.9

Source: Ministry of Finance and Economic Development (MoFED)

Table A.2: Sectorial Contribution to GDP and GDP Growth (in Million Birr)

Items		**Fiscal Year**				
		2007/08	2008/09	2009/10	2010/11	2011/12
Share in GDP (in %)	Agriculture	49.1	47.5	46.2	45.2	43.7
	Industry	10.2	10.2	10.2	10.5	11.0
	Services	41.3	42.8	43.8	44.2	45.3
Agriculture	Contribution to GDP growth	3.7	3.0	3.5		
	Contribution in%	32.7	30.2	33.4		
	Absolute Growth	7.4	6.4	7.6	9.0	4.9
Industry	Contribution to GDP growth	1.0	1.0	1.1		
	Contribution in%	9.4	9.7	10.5		
	Absolute Growth	10.3	9.6	10.8	14.9	13.6

Service	Contribution to GDP growth	6.6	6.0	5.8		
	Contribution in%	59.3	59.8	54.6	48.8	58.4
	Absolute Growth	16.1	14.0	13.2	12.6	11.1

Source: Ministry of Finance and Economic Development (MoFED)

Note: Sectoral contributions do not add-up to overall GDP growth because of Financial Intermediary Service Indirect Measurement (FISIM).

Table A.3: Definition on Bank Performance Measurement Parameter

Parameters	**Formula**
Overall Profitability	
Profit Margin	(Net income / total income)*100
ROA	Net income in year t / [(Asset in year t + Asset in year t-1)/2] *100
ROE	Net income in year t / [(Capital in year t + Capital in year t-1)/2] *100
Share of credit service in overall profitability	
Interest income / Gross revenue	
Net Interest Margin	Net interest income / the value of interest bearing assets
Pricing	
Net Interest spread	[interest income / value of interest bearing assets] - [interest expense/ value of interest paying liabilities]

Economies of Scale (Efficiency)	
Administrative cost / disbursement	Administrative cost / disbursement *100
Quality of Loans	
Provision for bad loan / outstanding loan	Provision for bad loan / outstanding loan *100

Source: *National Bank of Ethiopia*

APPENDIX B: CSA MANUFACTURING INDUSTRY SURVEY

Table B.1: Number of Manufacturing Enterprises (Population size)

Years	Micro (0-9)	Small (10-20)	Medium (21-99)	Large (100+)	Total
2005	2	404	136	207	749
2006	4	700	179	224	1,107
2007	3	881	165	236	1,285
2008	5	1,191	195	264	1,655
2009	44	1,264	193	274	1,775
2010	102	1,168	243	374	1,887
2011	35	1,253	242	332	1,862

Source: CSA survey data 2005-2012 and author's calculations

Note: This sample size is before outliers. Sample size in regressions differs due to non-response for key variable

Table B.2: Number of Manufacturing SMEs (Sample Size)

Years	Small (10-20)	Medium (21-99)	Total
2005	404	136	540
2006	700	179	879
2007	881	165	1046
2008	1,191	195	1386
2009	1,264	193	1457
2010	1,168	243	1411
2011	1,253	242	1495

Source: CSA of Ethiopia manufacturing survey data 2005-2012 and author's calculations

Table B.3: Number of manufacturing enterprises observations

Size category	Ownership	Age	Number of

	category	category	observations
Medium	Public	Young	58
		Old	255
	Private	Young	317
		Old	177
Small	Public	Young	18
		Old	55
	Private	Young	372
		Old	647

Source: CSA of Ethiopia manufacturing survey data 2005-2012 and author's calculations

Table B.4: Key Problems Faced: Enterprise Perception

Major Problems Faced by the Enterprise	% of All Enterprises	% of Enterprises with Bank credit	% of Enterprises with no Bank credit
Shortage of supply of raw materials	34.46	33.16	35.39
Getting market/customers	14.55	10.23	17.63
Shortage of working capital	7.27	6.53	7.81
Inconvenient working place	2.28	2.39	2.39
Government rules and regulation	3.23	2.82	3.53
No problems faced	3.82	3.88	3.78
others	34.39	40.99	29.47

Source: CSA of Ethiopia manufacturing survey data 2005-2012 and author's calculations

Table B.5: Patterns in Raw Material Use and Sources

	Share of Raw Materials in Value of Sales (%)	% of Enterprises Importing Raw Materials

Enterprises with Bank credit	51.11	65.05
Enterprises without Bank credit	53.49	48.28

Source: CSA of Ethiopia manufacturing survey data 2005-2012 and author's calculations

Table B.6: Manufacturing industries and respective share of value-added

Industrial group	% of firms (of total no. of firms)		% share of value added		% share of Employment	
	2005/06	2009/10	2005/06	2009/10	2005/10	2009/10
Food and beverage	29.90	26.30	40.38	34.95	30.12	32.48
Non-metallic minerals	12.20	22.20	15.70	19.24	8.52	10.53
Metal Products	8.50	7.00	3.04	6.93	6.68	5.78
Paper and paper products	7.00	5.66	5.35	4.89	6.81	5.40
Leather	5.06	5.24	4.37	2.34	1.79	2.17
Rubber and Plastic	5.00	6.40	8.87	7.38	5.83	7.49
Chemicals	4.30	4.40	4.86	8.10	4.79	6.04
Textiles	3.30	1.85	3.41	6.26	18.66	11.55
Basic Iron and Steel	1.40	1.80	3.92	1.52	4.90	5.39
Others	23.34	19.15	10.1	8.42	11.9	13.17

Source: CSA of Ethiopia manufacturing survey data 2005-2012 and author's calculations

APPENDIX C: GENERAL SMEs PRODUCTIVITY ESTIMATION RESULTS

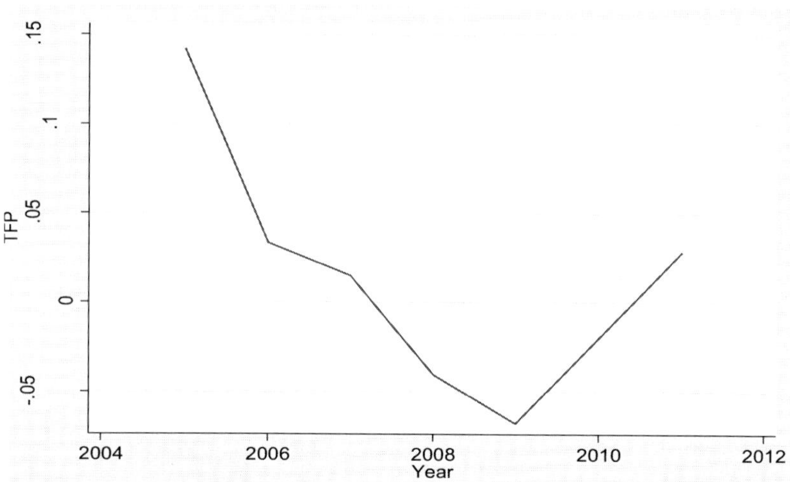

Figure C.1: The trend of SMEs TFP between year 2005 and 2007

Source: CSA of Ethiopia manufacturing survey data 2005-2012 and author's calculations

The graph shows that the trend of TFP is such that it steadily decreased between year 2005 and 2007 and then sharply increased after words.

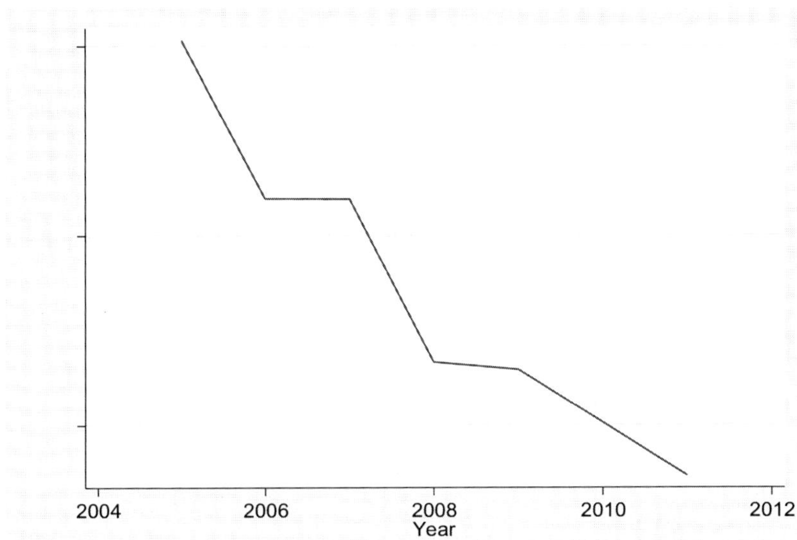

Figure C.2: Trends of SMEs Output with respect to years (2005 to 2012)

Source: CSA of Ethiopia manufacturing survey data 2005-2012 and author's calculations

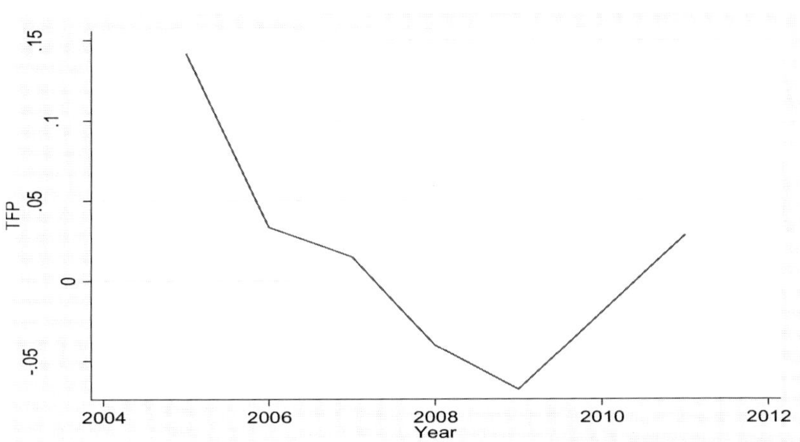

Figure C.3: The trend of enterprises TFP (total factor productivity)

Source: CSA of Ethiopia manufacturing survey data 2005-2012 and author's calculations

Note: The trend of TFP is such that it steadily decreased between year 2005 and 2007 and then sharply increased after words.

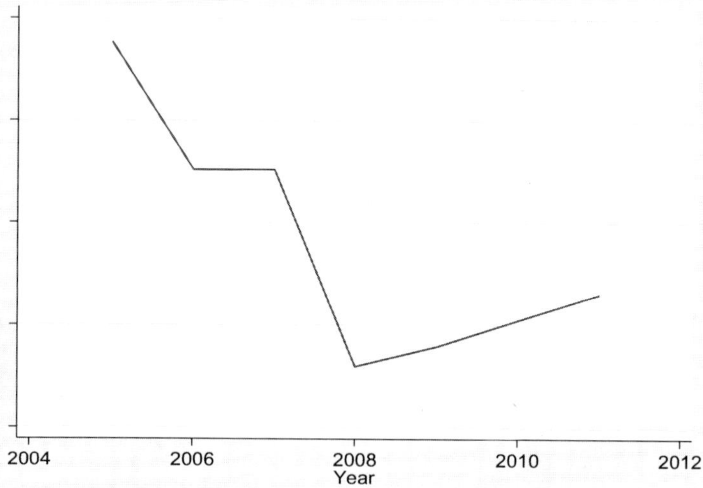

Figure C.4: Trends of SMEs Profit with respect to years (2005-2012)

Source: CSA of Ethiopia manufacturing survey data 2005-2012 and author's calculations

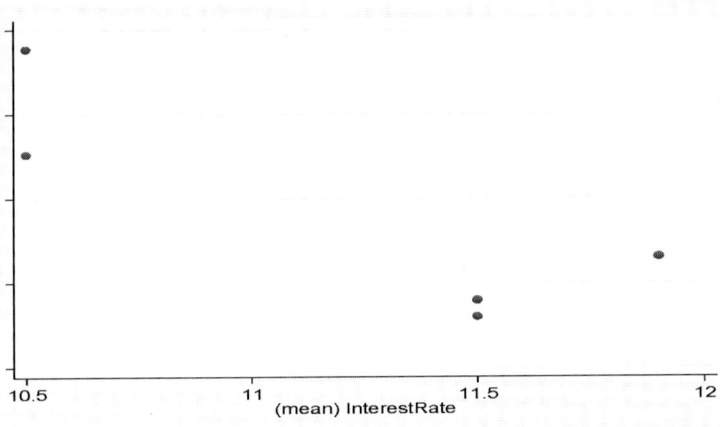

Figure C.5: Trends of SME Profit with respect to interest payment over the years 2005-2012.

Source: CSA of Ethiopia manufacturing survey data 2005-2012 and author's calculations

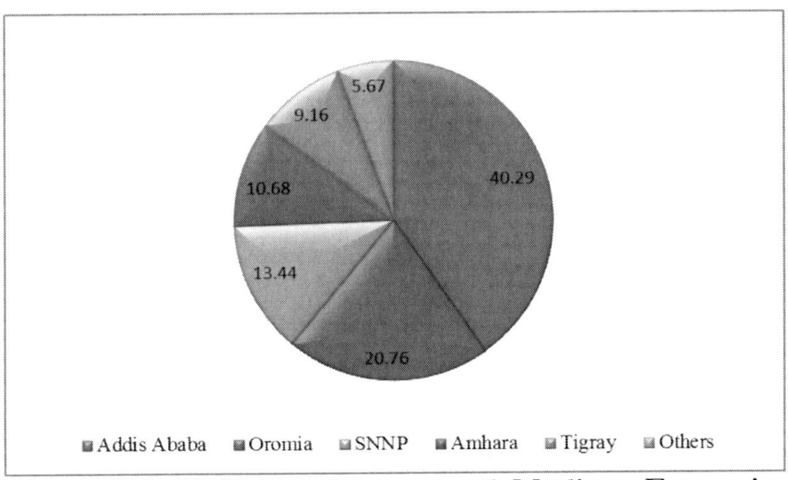

Figure C.6: % Share of Large and Medium Enterprises Establishment by Region

Source: CSA of Ethiopia manufacturing survey data 2005-2012 and author's calculations

Most establishments are located in urban areas and are not evenly distributed over the country, with Addis Ababa and Oromia region taking the largest share.

APPENDIX D: REGRESSION RESULTS

1. The basic Model (Model 1)

1.1. Production function estimated using the variables capital, labour, raw materials, energy and other industrial inputs.

Table D.1: Production function estimated using the variables capital, labour, raw materials

Output	Coef.	Std. Err.	T	P>|t|	[95% Conf. Interval]	
ln_capitalt-1	.0232378	.0042691	5.44	0.000	.0148684	.0316073
ln_waget-1	.1852013	.0092624	19.99	0.000	.1670424	.203360
ln_materialt-1	.7169264	.0073499	97.54	0.000	.702517	.7313359
Constant	1.98062	.0981002	20.19	0.000	1.788296	2.172945

Source: CSA of Ethiopia manufacturing survey data 2005-2012 and author's calculations

The results indicate that the model F(3,4524) = 5871.67; Prob. =.000<.01) is highly significant, and capital (Prob. =.000<.01), labour (Prob.=.000) and raw materials (Prob.=.000<.01) are highly significant at the 1% level.

Fixed-effects (within) regression Number of obs = 7365

Group variable: Enterprise ID Number of groups = 2758

R-sq: within = 0.6628 Obs per group: min = 1, Between = 0.8760 avg = 2.7

Overall = 0.8807 max = 6, F(6,4601) = 1507.33, corr(u_i, Xb) = 0.4378 Prob > F = 0.0000

Table D.2: model 2, raw materials and capital were lamped together

Output	Coef.	Std. Err.	t	P>|t|	[95% Conf. Interval]	
Lamped inputs	.7620509	.0111946	68.07	0.000	.7401042	.7839977
2006	.1183011	.023841	-4.96	0.000	.1650409	-.0715613
2007	-.1711872	.0241556	-7.09	0.000	-.2185438	-.1238307
2008	-.4460323	.0239726	-18.61	0.000	-.4930301	-.3990345
2009	-.4696224	.0247958	-18.94	0.000	-.5182341	-.4210108
2011	-1.182195	.0244315	-48.39	0.000	-1.230092	-1.134297
Constant	3.211605	.1585041	20.26	0.000	2.900861	3.522349

Source: CSA of Ethiopia manufacturing survey data 2005-2012 and author's calculations

sigma_u | .7461081, sigma_e | .46274956, rho | .72219364 (fraction of variance due to u_i)

F test that all u_i=0: F(2757, 4601) = 5.10 Prob > F = 0.0000

Table D.3: model 3, raw materials and capital were lamped together

Output	**Coef.**	**Std. Err.**	**t**	**P>|t|**	**[95% Conf. Interval]**	
ln_capitalt-1	.0179855	.0042102	4.27	0.000	.0097313	.0262396
ln_waget-1	.1156831	.0103723	11.15	0.000	.0953484	.1360178
ln_materialt-1	.7009664	.0074005	94.72	0.000	.6864579	.715475
Year						
2006	-.1060606	.0182265	-5.82	0.000	-.1417934	-.0703278
2007	-.1104351	.0183853	-6.01	0.000	-.1464793	-.074391
2008	-.1974566	.0184401	-10.71	0.000	-.2336082	-.1613049
2009	-.1157197	.0189614	-6.10	0.000	-.1528932	-.0785461
2011	-.3210882	.0227232	-14.13	0.000	-.3656367	-.2765397
Constant	3.184414	.1305831	24.39	0.000	2.928407	3.440421

Source: CSA of Ethiopia manufacturing survey data 2005-2012 and author's calculations

Table D.4: Model 3, dummies were therefore created and were included in the model.

	Coef.	Std. Err.	t	P>|t|	[95% Conf. Interval]	
Capital	.0179428	.0042106	4.26	0.000	.009688	.0261975
Labour	.1156702	.0103725	11.15	0.000	.095335	.1360054
Raw materials	.7011239	.0074011	94.73	0.000	.6866141	.7156338
2006	-.1058752	.018217	-5.81	0.000	-.1415894	-.070161
2007	-.1102624	.0183758	-6.00	0.000	-.146288	-.0742367
2008	-.1973698	.0184351	-10.71	0.000	-.2335116	-.161228
2009	-.1155374	.018951	-6.10	0.000	-.1526907	-.0783842
2011	-.3208314	.0227114	-14.13	0.000	-.3653567	-.276306
Constant	3.182853	.1305525	24.38	0.000	2.926907	3.4388

Source: CSA of Ethiopia manufacturing survey data 2005-2012 and author's calculations

Note: F test that all u_i=0: F (2681, 4519) = 3.52 Prob > F = 0.0000 R-sq: within = 0.8014

Though according to Baltagi, cross-sectional dependence is a problem in macro panels with long time series or over 20-30 years, and so, this would not be much of a problem in micro panels (with few years and large number of cases) like this one, cross-sectional dependence or heteroscedasticity is tested. The null hypothesis in the B-P/LM test of independence is that residuals across entities were not correlated. The following were the random-effects model results

Table D.5: Model 3, dummies included in the model.

Output |	Coef.	Std. Err.	t	P>|t|	[95% Conf. Interval]	
Capital	.0181674	.0045213	4.02	0.000	.0093032	.0270316
Labour	.1135879	.0113765	9.98	0.000	.0912838	.1358919
Raw materials	.6991469	.0079044	88.45	0.000	.68365	.7146437
2006	-.1125746	.0188684	-5.97	0.000	-.1495668	-.0755825
2007	-.1116635	.0190516	-5.86	0.000	-.1490147	-.0743122
2008	.2000243	.0192216	-10.41	0.000	-.2377089	-.1623397

2009	-.1176818	.0199841	-5.89	0.000	-.1568613	-.0785022
2011	-.2995051	.0265354	-11.29	0.000	-.3515286	-.2474815
Age	-.0003254	.0010252	-0.32	0.751	-.0023354	.0016845
Type of owner	.0268923	.0259663	1.04	0.300	-.0240155	.0778001
Size of business	-1.28e-06	.0000467	-0.03	0.978	-.0000928	.0000902
Region3	-.0029157	.1074276	-0.03	0.978	-.2135312	.2076998
Region4	-.1145971	.0956832	-1.20	0.231	-.3021874	.0729932
Region 7	.0929129	.1107985	0.84	0.402	-.1243114	.3101372
Region 13	-.0289168	.1513198	-0.19	0.848	-.3255847	.2677511
Region 14	-.0940711	.0878172	-1.07	0.284	-.2662398	.0780976
Region 15	-.0705051	.130377	-0.54	0.589	-.3261139	.1851036
Constant	3.283734	.164216	20.00	0.000	2.961782	3.605685

Source: CSA of Ethiopia manufacturing survey data 2005-2012 and author's calculations

Fixed-effects (within) regression Number of obs = 6772
Group variable: enterprise ID Number of groups = 2603
R-sq: within = 0.7662 Obs per group: min = 1, between = 0.9433 avg = 2.6
overall = 0.9401 max = 6, F(12,4157) = 1135.09, corr(u_i, Xb) = 0.4346 Prob > F = 0.0000

Table D.6: Model 3, Time-effects dummies included in the model.

Output |	Coef.	Std. Err.	t	P>|t|	[95% Conf. Interval]	
Capital	.0228719	.0045584	5.02	0.000	.0139349	.0318089
Labour	.1677416	.0105091	15.96	. 0.000	.1471381	.1883451
Raw materials	.7066097	.0079061	. 89.38	0.000	.6911095	.7221099

Age	-.0029436	.0009996	-2.94	0.003	-.0049033	-.0009839
Type of owner	.0212525	.0263594	. 0.81	0.420	-.0304259	.072931
Size of business	.0000648	.0000463	1.40	. 0.162	-.0000259	.0001555
Region3	.0194881	.1095471	0.18	. 0.859	-.1952828	.2342591
Region4	-.0974228	.0975165	-1.00	0.318	-.2886073	.0937618
Region 7	.1061574	.1130325	. 0.94	0.348	-.1154469	.3277616
Region 13	-.0475086	.1543503	-0.31	0.758	-.3501178	.2551006
Region 14	-.083176	.0895028	-0.93	-0.93	0.353	-.2586493
Region 15	-.0456106	.1329954	-0.34	0.732	-.3063527	.2151316
Constant	2.417875	.1464353	16.51	0.000	0.000	2.130783

Source: CSA of Ethiopia manufacturing survey data 2005-2012 and author's calculations

sigma_u | .49898822, sigma_e | .36075771, rho | .65672914 (fraction of variance due to u_i) F test that all u_i=0: F(2602, 4157) = 3.25 Prob > F = 0.0000, It should be noted that when the time fixed effects were removed from the model, the Age coefficient became highly significant (Prob.=.003<.01).

Table D.7: Production function estimated using variables capital, labor, and raw materials

Output	Coef.	Std. Err.	z	P>|z|	[95% Conf. Interval]	
ln_capital	.0394702	.0030986	12.74	0.000	.033397	.0455433
ln_wage	.2026623	.006243	32.46	0.000	.1904264	.2148983
ln_material	.732051	.0049755	147.13	0.000	.7222991	.7418028
2006	-.1009794	.0178864	-5.65	0.000	-.1360362	-.0659227
2007	-.1113955	.0178881	-6.23	0.000	-.1464555	-.0763355
2008	-.1690412	.0175887	-9.61	0.000	-.2035145	-.1345679
2009	-.0979207	.0176268	-5.56	0.000	-.1324686	-.0633728
2011	-.1624585	.0192738	-8.43	0.000	-.2002345	-.1246825
Constant	1.477836	.0551047	26.82	0.000	1.369833	1.585839

Source: CSA of Ethiopia manufacturing survey data 2005-2012 and author's calculations F(8,2681) = 1194.18 corr (ui, Xb) = 0.5538,

Prob > F = 0.0000. The results indicate cross-sectional dependence and so heteroscedasticity in the data. The "frees" test is not performed due to having insufficient observations. In order to counteract the effect of the dependence, robust standard errors were used to estimate the regression model as follows.

Table D.8: Robust standard errors to estimate the regression model

Output	Coef.	Std. Err.	t	P>|t|	[95% Conf. Interval]	
ln_capital	.0179428	.0057427	3.12	0.002	.0066821	.0292034
ln_wage	.1156702	.0205309	5.63	0.000	.0754122	.1559283
ln_material	.7011239	.0272676	25.71	0.000	.6476563	.7545916
2006/07	-.1058752	.0172917	-6.12	0.000	-.1397816	-.0719687
2007/08	-.1102624	.018356	-6.01	0.000	-.1462557	-.074269
2008/09	-.1973698	.0195854	-10.08	0.000	-.2357739	-.1589657
2009/10	-.1155374	.0195313	-5.92	0.000	-.1538354	-.0772395
2011/12	-.3208314	.0358299	-8.95	0.000	-.3910884	-.2505743
Constant	3.182853	.3477261	9.15	0.000	2.501015	3.864692

Source: CSA of Ethiopia manufacturing survey data 2005-2012 and author's calculations

Table D.9: Production function estimated using variables capital, labour, raw materials, energy and other industrial inputs.

	1 **with Loan**	**2** **without Loan**
ln_capital	0.0449*** (4.73)	0.0673*** (6.25)
ln_material	0.618*** (45.89)	0.599*** (45.53)
ln_wage	0.215*** (11.87)	0.179*** (11.73)
ln_energy	0.0750*** (5.92)	0.0888** *(6.98)

ln_otherin~s	0.0574*** (5.19)	0.0380*** (3.67)
_cons	1.546***	2.011***
N	565	729
R-sq	0.963	0.943

Source: CSA of Ethiopia manufacturing survey data 2005-2012 and author's calculations

t statistics in parentheses, * $p<0.05$, ** $p<0.01$, *** $p<0.001$

Table D.10: T –test on the difference in mean TFP across enterprises with and without Bank credit.

Variable	Obs	Mean	Std. Err	Std Dev.	[95% Conf. Interval]
no	812	8.319498	.2689347	7.663458	7.791608 8.847388
Yes	598	5.144429	.1573912	3.84885	4.835321 5.453537
combined	1410	6.972908	.1737037	6.522568	6.632163 7.313654
Diff		3.175069	.3116053		2.563747 3.786391

Source: CSA of Ethiopia manufacturing survey data 2005-2012 and author's calculations

diff = mean(no) - mean(yes) t = 10.1894, Ho: diff = 0 Satterthwaite's degrees of freedom = 1260.77, Ha: diff < 0 Ha: diff! = 0 Ha: diff > 0, Pr(T < t) = 1.0000 Pr(|T| > |t|) = 0.0000 Pr(T > t) = 0.0000. Note: - "yes" and "no" refer to enterprises with and without access respectively.

Table D.11: Production function estimated using the same procedure with capital and raw material lumped together

	1 with Loan	2 without Loan
ln_capital	0.684***	0.686***

	(31.90)	(38.31)
ln_wage	0.226*** (9.13)	0.166*** (9.22)
ln_energy	0.0348 (1.96)	0.0354* (2.33)
ln_otherin~s	0.0578*** (3.82)	0.0553*** (4.52)
_cons	1.038*** (5.16)	1.807*** (11.36)
N R-sq	566 0.931	738 0.918

Source: CSA of Ethiopia manufacturing survey data 2005-2012 and author's calculations

t statistics in parentheses, * $p<0.05$, ** $p<0.01$, *** $p<0.001$

Table D.12: T-test on the difference in mean TFP across enterprises with and without access to credit.

Variable.	Obs	Mean	Std. Err	Std Dev.	[95% Conf. Interval]
no	812	6.772113	.13176	3.754582	6.513483 7.030744
Yes	598	3.156155	.0602267	1.472785	3.037873 3.274437
combined	1410	5.238537	.0931284	3.496967	5.055851 5.421222
Diff		3.615959		.1448722	3.331707 3.900211

Source: CSA of Ethiopia manufacturing survey data 2005-2012 and author's calculations diff = mean (no) – mean (yes) t = 24.9597, Ho: diff = 0 Satterthwaite's degrees of freedom = 1118.94, Ha: diff < 0 Ha: diff! = 0 Ha: diff > 0, Pr(T < t) = 1.0000 Pr(|T| > |t|) = 0.0000 Pr(T > t) = 0.0000

Table D.13: Estimation of production function using basic model and control variables

	1 with Loan	2 without Loan
ln_capital	0.0460***	0.0704***
ln_material	0.629*** (40.44)	0.600*** (40.96)
ln_wage	0.215*** (9.52)	0.194*** (10.90)
ln_energy	0.0680*** (4.59)	0.0997*** (6.70)
ln_otherin~s	0.0502*** (3.98)	0.0213 (1.88)
_Iregion_2	1.198** (3.00)	0.0564 (0.30)
_Iregion_3	-0.0528 (-0.61)	-0.213*** (-3.31)
_Iregion_4	0.0193 (0.25)	-0.143* (-2.39)
_Iregion_5	-0.0109 (-0.06)	-0.233 (-0.59)
_Iregion_6	-0.0610 (-0.33)	0.271 (0.68)
_Iregion_7	-0.0277 (-0.31)	-0.155** (-2.66)
_Iregion_12	-0.335 (-0.88)	-0.167 (-0.79)
_Iregion_13	0.117 (0.56)	-0.326** (-3.12)
_Iregion_14	0.0289 (0.40)	-0.0532 (-0.91)
_Iregion_15	0.0292 (0.22)	-0.252* (-2.38)

Source: CSA of Ethiopia manufacturing survey data 2005-2012 and author's calculations
Note: Coefficients on number of years in business are not reported; too many values.

These conclusions are viewed as the foundation for conducting research on the impact of bank credit on SME productivity and profitability in Ethiopia.

091221-100-1-60W

INDEX

INDEX

091221-100-1-60W